We Hold These Truths

What America Means to Me

COMPILED AND EDITED BY
SUSAN CHEEVES KING

Scripture references marked ESV are take from *The Holy Bible, English Standard Version*. ESV® Text Edition: 2016. Copyright © 2001 by Crossway Bibles, a publishing ministry of Good News Publishers. All rights reserved. Used by permission.

Scripture references marked KJV are taken from the *New American Standard Bible*, 1995 Copyright © 1960, 1962, 1963, 1968, 1971, 1972, 1973, 1975, 1977, 1995 by The Lockman Foundation, La Habra, CA. All rights reserved. Used by permission.

Scripture references marked NET are taken from *The Net Bible*, *New English Translation Bible* copyright ©1996-2017 by Biblical Studies Press, L.L.C. All rights reserved. Used by permission.

Scripture references marked NIV are taken from *The Holy Bible, New International Version*®, NIV® Copyright ©1973, 1978, 1984, 2011 by Biblica, Inc.® Used by permission. All rights reserved worldwide.

Scripture references marked NKJV taken from the *New King James Version*®. Copyright © 1982 by Thomas Nelson. Used by permission. All rights reserved.

Scripture references marked NLT are taken from *Holy Bible, New Living Translation*, copyright © 1996, 2004, 2015 by Tyndale House Foundation. Used by permission of Tyndale House Publishers, Inc., Carol Stream, Illinois 60188. All rights reserved. Used by permission.

Royalties for this book are donated to World Christian Broadcasting.

WE HOLD THESE TRUTHS
   WHAT AMERICA MEANS TO ME

ISBN-13: 978-1-60495-099-1

Copyright © 2024 by Grace Publishing House. Published in the U.S.A. by Grace Publishing House. All rights reserved. No part of this book may be reproduced in any form or by any electronic or mechanical means, including information storage and retrieval systems, without permission in writing, except as provided by U.S.A. Copyright law.

Table of Contents

INTRODUCTION 6
1. *400 Years in 800 Words . . . ~* Bonnie Evans 9
2. *In God We Trust ~* Cristina Moore 13
THE ARMY GOES ROLLING ALONG 16
3. *Earn This ~* Rachel Coggins 18
4. *A Fourth of July Story ~* Jeff Brady 20
5. *If You Can Keep It ~* Joanne Fleck 26
6. *Home of the American Brave in England ~* Pamela Cosel 28
WHEN JOHNNY COMES MARCHING HOME ~ Parick Gilmore 34
7. *No Land? ~* Lillian Joyce 36
8. *A Call to Act ~* Alice H. Murray 39
9. *Look Past World War II ~* Carol Baird 42
10. *A Young Land Put to the Test ~* Russell MacClaren 45
THE STAR-SPANGLED BANNER ~FRANCIS SCOTT KEY 47
11. *Why I Fly the Flag ~* Desiree St. Clair Spears 49
12. *What 9/11 Taught Me About My Country ~* Beverly Robertson 52
13. *They Show Us What a Patriot Is ~* Judson I. Stone 54
14. *Liberty Sleeps ~* Jennifer Cotney 58
15. *Glad to Devote My Life ~* Eddie Burchfield 60
THE U.S. AIR FORCE SONG 62
16. *Love of Country ~* Leah Hinton 64
OVER THERE ~ GEORGE M. COHAN 67
17. *A Flag, a Prayer, and a Journey Home ~* Penny L. Hunt 68
18. *The Over-and-Above Patriot ~* Jasmine Gatti 70
BATTLE HYMN OF THE REPUBLIC ~ JULIA WARD HOWE 73

19. *Patriotic by Nature?* ~ Pam Groves 75
20. *The Capitol Remains* ~ Jeff Brady 77
21. *View From a Far Land* ~ Debra Kornfield 80
22. *A True Patriot* ~ Lin Daniels 83
23. *I Love America* ~ Debbie Jansen 85
YANKEE DOODLE BOY ~ GEORGE M. COHAN (1904) 88
24. *These Things We Hold Dear* ~ Kenneth Avon White 90
25. *I Am Free* ~ Michelle Newman 93
26. *Home of the Free and the Brave* ~ Liz Kimmel 97
27. *My Uncle George* ~ Michael Shoemaker 100
ANCHORS AWEIGH 102
28. *Just a Patriot* ~ Jim Layton 103
29. *My United States* ~ Allyson West Lewis 105
30. *Much Left to Love* ~ Susan Cheeves King 107
YOU'RE A GRAND OLD FLAG 114
31. *The Real National Treasure* ~ John Leatherman 116
32. *This Is America to Me* ~ Heather Holbrook 118
33. *One Proud Marine* ~ Glenda Ferguson 120
IN FLANDERS FIELD 123
THE MARINES' HYMN 124
34. *The Heart of a Nation* ~ Terry Magness 125
35. *Land of the Free, Paid for by the Brave* ~ Jan White 128
36. *My Pledge* ~ Karen Masteller 130
37. *The Heart of America* ~ Kim Robinson 132
AMERICA THE BEAUTIFUL 135
38. *What Patriotism Means to Me* ~ Patricia Huey 137
DECLARATION OF INDEPENDENCE (EXCERPTS) 141
THE U.S. CONSTITUTION PREAMBLE 143
THE U.S. BILL OF RIGHTS 144
THE GETTYSBURG ADDRESS 147
ABOUT THE AUTHORS 148

Dedication

To all those who risk their lives
running toward danger for the sake of others
and to those who make it possible for them to do so

Introduction

When we sent the callout for submissions for this book, we didn't intend for it to be focused on those who have served in the American military. But, on the other hand, we shouldn't have been surprised that so much of what we received would do just that. I think all patriots would agree that the height of patriotism is to be willing to die for one's country. Abraham Lincoln referred to this ultimate sacrifice as he dedicated the cemetery at Gettysburg in 1863: "They gave the last *full measure of devotion.*" Jesus Christ phrased it this way: *"Greater love has no one than this, that someone lay down his life for his friends"* (John 15:13 ESV).

The focus on those in military service also brings to mind a notable characteristic of our national character — the singular way we do war. Most of the time our sense of compassion and decency is what has led America to come to the aid of nations under attack. Unlike super powers throughout history, our goal in entering a war has never been to conquer other countries. An interchange between Colin Powell and the Archbishop of Canterbury underscores this truth. To the Archbishop's accusatory question about empire building, Powell replied: "Over the years, the United States has sent many of its fine young men and women into great peril to fight for freedom beyond our borders. The only amount of land we have ever asked for in return is enough to bury those that did not return."

Another feature of this book is the very intentional decision to include within its pages some patriotic songs. Most of us know the power of music to "soothe the savage breast" but the words also have the power to seat deeply into the minds and hearts of all of us. This year at a D-day event in Normandy, those of us in the U.S.A. watched on our screens as a 99-year-old American veteran sang *God Bless America* with every word and every note right — and on key.

Lyrics can become so imprinted on us that it is not uncommon even for people with dementia to remember the songs of their youth. And doesn't every patriot's sense of loyalty and pride surge when they hear one of those inspiring songs about our wonderful country?

I remember the way my own patriotism was stirred as I watched so many of those old movies on Saturday mornings. A particular movie that resonated in my heart was *Yankee Doodle Dandy* (the George M. Cohan story) starring James Cagney. That's partly why we included two Cohan songs in this book. I used one of them to encourage love for our country within my two dear grandsons, starting when they were very small. Every time we saw a U.S. flag (quite often when we were on errands since one flies on the hill overlooking their neighborhood), we would sing the first verse of "You're a Grand Old Flag." By the age of two, each boy would make it a point to scan the skies for a flag and then start the song himself.

Unfortunately, we couldn't include all the songs we would have liked to — only those in the public domain. One of my favorites is "This Land is Your Land." Another I especially wish we had in this book will forever be linked in our minds to the way our whole country came together after 9/11: "God Bless the USA" by Lee Greenwood with its "proud to be an American" phrase and the one that always brings tears to my eyes: "And I'll gladly stand up next to you/And defend her still today."

I'm sure we all miss one particular song, *God Bless America*. "It's not a patriotic song," stated its composer, Irving Berlin, "but an expression of gratitude for what this country has done for its citizens, of what home really means."

Like the others before it, Book XIII in the *Short and Sweet* series is based on an assignment I've been giving writers at conferences for over 25 years when I teach them about learning to write with excellent style: "Write about something close to your heart using words of only one syllable."

I allow the writers seven exceptions to the one-syllable-word-only requirement. Trust me; if you see a polysyllabic word in any of these stories, it is because that word fits into one of those exceptions.

If you're a writer — or aspire to be — and the challenge of writing in words of (mostly) one syllable intrigues you, why not give it a try? Contact me at shortandsweettoo@gmail.com to obtain the upcoming theme and deadline. You could see your own work featured in the next book in the *Short and Sweet* series.

Susan Cheeves King

~ 1 ~
400 Years in 800 Words...

Bonnie Evans

Poor. Crushed. No hope.
They yearned to breathe free.
Ears heard hints of a New World.
Hope rose, dreams sparked.
Take a chance. Choose.
Board boat. Set sail.
Waves build. Ship rolls.
People sick. Two die. Two born.
Sail. Sail.
Sun up. Moon sinks. Many times.
Days. Weeks. Months.
Sail. Sail.
At last — by God's grace — land.
New land. Rich land. Our land.

... after many difficulties in boisterous storms, at length, by God's providence, we espied land which was deemed to be Cape Cod, and so afterward it proved. And the appearance of it much comforted us, especially seeing so goodly a land, and wooded to the brink of the sea. It caused us to rejoice together and praise God. (Journal of Plymouth Pilgrim, Edward Winslow, 1620).

Build. Plant. Plan.
Pacts. Deals. Vows.
Farms and forts.
Famine, disease, harsh cold, native foes . . .
but their feet tread the New World's floor,
so they breathe, hope, and dream.

Trade laws. Tolls. Tyranny.
Men step up to give the only thing they own:
Brave hearts.

Gentlemen may cry, 'Peace, Peace' — but, there is no peace. The war is actually begun! The next gale that sweeps from the north will bring to our ears the clash of resounding arms! Our brethren are already in the field! Why stand we here idle? What is it that gentlemen wish? What would they have? Is life so dear, or peace so sweet, as to be purchased at the price of chains and slavery? Forbid it, Almighty God! I know not what course others may take; but as for me, give me liberty or give me death!
Patrick Henry, 1775

War. On land. At sea.
Men die. More. Even more.
God sent His grace and the home-grown troops won.
Freedom's price: Paid In Full.

What Next?
Where do we go?
How can we grow?
Go west. Go up. Go over. Go across.

Wait! Men and women bought and sold.
How can this be in the land of the free?

Time to stand as one once more.
Choose to break the chains some wear.

The brave come from fields and towns.
They tote guns and march in dread.
Fathers and sons die where they fall.
Wives wear black. Mothers tend graves. Hearts rend.
States torn, families crushed, the land ruined.
Freedom's price flows red with grief.

Our movement may be one of severe conflict and death to me. Not my will, but thine, O God, be done. If it is necessary that I should fall on the battlefield for my country, I am ready. I have no misgivings about, or lack of confidence in, the cause in which I am engaged, and my courage does not halt or falter. I know how strongly American Civilization now leans upon the triumph of the Government, and how great a debt we owe to those who went before us through the blood and suffering of the Revolution. And I am willing — perfectly willing — to lay down all my joys in this life, to help maintain this Government, and to pay that debt.
   Sullivan, Union soldier, to his wife Sarah, 1861

Sarah, my love for you is deathless, it seems to bind me to you with mighty cables that nothing but Omnipotence could break; and yet my love of Country comes over me like a strong wind and bears me irresistibly on with all these chains to the battlefield. If I do not return, my dear Sarah, never forget how much I love you, and when my last breath escapes me on the battlefield, it will whisper your name."
   Sullivan, 1861

War ends. The wounds are great but freedom reigns for all.
Hearts heal. Hands reach.
Hope rises. Dreams spark.

From 1609 to 2024.
From 102 to 300 million.
From 13 to 50.

Now. Here. Heirs stand.
On grass. In weeds.
On decks. In drives. On hills.
By homes. In cars. On quilts.
Side by Side.
Look up.
Fire and light. Ash and beauty. War and peace.

Rejoice but also hold in your mind:
Honor the past.
Fan the flames of dreams not yet born.
Let hope rise and swell.
Choose to serve. Choose to be brave. Choose to be free.

It is for us, the living . . . to be dedicated here to the unfinished work which they who fought have thus far so nobly advanced. It is . . . for us to be here dedicated to the great task remaining before us — that from these honored dead we take increased devotion to that cause for which they gave the last full measure of devotion — that we here highly resolve that these dead shall not have died in vain — that this nation, under God, shall have a new birth of freedom — and that government of the people, by the people, for the people, shall not perish from the earth.
                    Abraham Lincoln, Gettysburg Address, 1863

~ 2 ~
In God We Trust

Cristina Moore

I can still smell the smoke from that day. The air was thick, and it was hard to breathe. I looked to the left and right of me, and all I saw were wrecked fire trucks, and on the ground, piles of torn blinds, bricks, and glass. In the tense quiet, I could hear an armed jet — the lone plane that flew that day. I stood in the midst of tragic loss up to my knees in piles of scraps made up of hand-drawn pics that just days before had hung in a place of work — gone in the blink of an eye. When I think of what America means to me, this is not the start of my tale but the point in time when the depth of my loyalty to this nation would never again be lost.

I was the first generation out of Puerto Rico where my mom was raised with nine brothers and sisters in a small home at the edge of a sugar-cane farm. While some saw the flaws in the United States when we came to this country, I saw the dreams that were made. I saw paths open to me. All I had to do was take the step.

By sixth grade I knew that I would join the military. I watched films like *Big Red One* and *Hamburger Hill* and knew that I had to be part of something more than me. From that point on, I was set in my goal, the path laid before me. All I had to do was take one step at a time. I began with straight As in school and joined track so I could be the best cadet candidate for West Point.

When I joined the Army, I found people with like minds who had heard the same call, a pull to serve this country that had given so much to us. Many of us found a home in the Army, a family that was not from blood but from shared grief and experiences. This family would stay with us, not because they had to, but because a bond was set that years apart would never break.

In the 29 years since I joined, that family has never failed me.

On the day our nation was hurt, I saw a country unite. I not only felt, but also saw what America means to me. As my husband and I drove from North Carolina to New York in our truck, we saw the strength in our neighbors along the way. The day after 9/11, we saw flags raised over each bridge and on the road to show each other that we still stood strong. When we made it to the heart of New York and began the walk of over 60 blocks to ground zero, we saw the streets lined with New Yorkers saying thank you. The rush to destroy our nation had failed. It brought us together in ways no one could have dreamed ahead of time. When we left, I knew I would never see my neighbor or this nation in the same way. I knew I would always see her hidden strength. I knew that I would never forget that she is worth fighting for, worth laying my life on the line time and time again. It has never been about me, but about what America means to me. She is my hope. She tells me — again and again — that when all seems against us, we stand as one.

I still serve in the Army and am now a mom of four kids. They, too, know what it means to serve, to be loyal, and to help others above self. It's the small things we do every day. It's when we share kind words even when they do not seem earned. It's when we spend a day to ship a box to soldiers far from home. It's when we hold our hand tight to our chest at the first notes of our anthem. Our kids have known war, when mom and dad had to leave for a year at a time. They know what this nation means and what it means to keep her safe. The theme in our home is to lead with love, to never lose sight that we are all God's children, that our nation was built on God in whom we trust, and it is God who will not leave us.

Of late, some have been led to ask if our nation has lost its hope, if we can't find our faith and have strayed far away. But I just think back to that day, when I stood at ground zero after a walk of over 60 blocks — every block with tears down my cheeks, not because of the loss but because of the hope that lined those city blocks.

That is what America means to me.

The Army Goes Rolling Along

March along, sing our song, with the Army of the free
Count the brave, count the true, who have fought to victory
We're the Army and proud of our name
We're the Army and proudly proclaim

First to fight for the right,
And to build the Nation's might,
And The Army Goes Rolling Along
Proud of all we have done,
Fighting till the battle's won,
And the Army Goes Rolling Along.

Then it's Hi! Hi! Hey!
The Army's on its way.
Count off the cadence loud and strong (TWO! THREE!)
For where e'er we go,
You will always know
That The Army Goes Rolling Along.

Valley Forge, Custer's ranks,
San Juan Hill and Patton's tanks,
And the Army went rolling along
Minute men, from the start,
Always fighting from the heart,
And the Army keeps rolling along.

Then it's Hi! Hi! Hey!
The Army's on its way.
Count off the cadence loud and strong (TWO! THREE!)
For where e'er we go,
You will always know
That The Army Goes Rolling Along.

Men in rags, men who froze,
Still that Army met its foes,
And the Army went rolling along.
Faith in God, then we're right,
And we'll fight with all our might,
As the Army keeps rolling along.

Then it's Hi! Hi! Hey!
The Army's on its way.
Count off the cadence loud and strong (TWO! THREE!)
For where e'er we go,
You will always know
That The Army Goes Rolling Along.

~ 3 ~
Earn This

Rachel Coggins

In the film *Saving Private Ryan,* Tom Hanks plays an Army officer sent to the front line of battle in World War II. His job is to bring Ryan home. The duty is not easy, and the hero is killed. As he dies, he looks at Ryan and says two words: "Earn this."

I get it. In the 25 years I served as an Army Reserve Chaplain I saw much grief and pain. I worked at Landstuhl Regional Medical Center (LRMC) in Landstuhl, Germany, during Operation Iraqi Freedom/Enduring Freedom. Those with war wounds were sent to LRMC straight from Iraq and Afghanistan. During the 12 months I was there in 2004-2005, some 12,000 troops came through. For many of them, their lives were changed for all time.

I was left with a strong sense that we must hold dear the price paid by these warriors. The phrase "earn this" sounds in my ears. Those who gave life and limb, who made us able to march in streets or rest in safe homes, need our full respect. It is a duty we cannot shirk. President John F. Kennedy told us, "Ask not what your country can do for you — ask what you can do for your country." I agree. Patriots are duty-bound to add value to the land we love.

The Army Creed led me through my Army tour and can

be a guide for all Americans. It tasks us to be part of a team and to serve and live with these values: loyalty, duty, respect, selfless service, honor, integrity, and personal courage. It goes on to tell us not to quit, to be tough in body and mind, and to train to be good at what we do. The creed ends with this line: "I will guard freedom and the American way of life."

Some would shame us for our past and strive to tear down what we have built. It hurts to see such angst in our country, yet I will not be shamed. With pride, I still will seek to earn what we have been given.

As a patriot and a Christian, I am led by this Bible verse: *Let us not become weary in doing good, for at the proper time we will reap a harvest if we do not give up* (Galatians 6:9 NIV). This patriot will stand firm and not tire in her love and care for the United States. I will stay the course and pray with hope that we "earn this" right to reap God's good will.

~ 4 ~
A Fourth of July Story

Jeff Brady

When I was young, we called it "Fourth of July" not Independence Day.

And it was all about Fireworks — both safe and sane ones and those I bought from some shady source I will not name. To my shame, it was not about those who gave up all their goods — and even their lives — for the sake of our country.

Since the age of nine or ten, I had been the host of a "Fourth of July" fireworks party at my house in Fremont, California. The site where we would make merry was our church parking lot next to my house.

I was a little kid, so I could work only part-time, but I would save up through the year to drop all of my cash at the Red Devil Fireworks stand (and also spend it with seedy hookups for "the good stuff").

This story took place the summer I turned 15. While the year is a bit fuzzy, the events are burned into my mind.

All my friends came, each with his stash of fireworks. As soon as it got dark, the havoc began.

I had turned my nest egg into a primo mix of — to quote my friend Joe — "whistlin' bungholes, spleen splitters, whisker biscuits, honkey lighters, hoosker doos, hoosker don'ts, cherry bombs, nipsy daisers (with or without the scooter stick) and whistlin' kitty chasers."

With great care, I laid out all the legal and other fireworks in the big box that I got at the Red Devil stand. I had placed them in their earned-power order: legal and "kiddy" fireworks first, "modified" legal fireworks next, and then "flying and blow-up" stuff. The finale would be a Frankenstein Firework that I jerry-rigged from a bunch of odds and ends, which was bound to breach the SALT II Agreements. (I mean, I did have an Estes Model Rocket engine on the thing.)

I was ready.

My Dad usually stood by for the start of the event to make sure we were not being idiots. But we were at least smart enough to delay the idiot acts until he left.

At least that was the usual plan.

But not that year.

Which is what makes this a story to still share 40 years later.

I was in my groove, ready for a long blow out of planned and sorted fireworks to occur in the ideal order. If we'd had Excel back then, I would have had a spreadsheet of what would take off and when.

I "prepped" by having a Jolt Cola — "All of the sugar, and twice the caffeine!"

I. Was. Ready.

It wasn't even fully dark when we kicked it off. As just a tease of what was to come, we lit some smoke pots and the "free" stuff they tossed-in when you spent $20 or more.

Then the worst came to pass.

One of us, I won't say who, cracked open a pack of sparklers.

Sparklers. The things you give little kids, and which are thought to be as safe as safe can get.

In truth they should be thought of as a Class 4 Hazard and sold only to *licensed professionals.*

Which we were not.

The person not named then lit the whole pack of sparklers, causing him to fade out of sight in the blast of spark and flame that lit up Freemont's Centerville District.

That is when things went into slow motion.

With an arc of light and speed, the sparklers dropped down a few feet and then shot into the sky, to break apart on their way up like a reverse-meteor that has crashed against the ether.

They stood still for a beat as the toss lost boost against the pull of gravity. This is when my brain caught on that some stuff might be amiss.

Like a pet cat taken out for the first time in its life, I stood there aghast, open-jawed, and wide-eyed as the sparklers began their fall back to earth.

The toss by the no-name person had placed them over a tree, and as they fell down through the tree each bounced off a branch or two like rocks aglow that are spit out by a volcano.

As a ball in a pachinko machine, the fiery rods of death jinked and jived their way down the tree toward the trunk, where I had placed my Box of Pyrotechnic Treasures to keep them safe from any flame.

I stood stock still with fear.

On the other hand, the sparklers could move with ease.

The tick and tock moves they made as they pinballed down

each branch were matched by a truly grand light show that, by some type of magic, did not catch the tree on fire.

Some burned out. Some fell to the ground, no harm done.

But one — one crazy, demon-owned super-sparkler that I assume was part of the Nazis' Super Weapons Program — seemed to pulse with even more bright light and send sparks far away as it reached the trunk of the tree.

With a final "tink" it hit the last branch and spun through space to bounce off of the edge of the box that held my hard-earned cache of gunpowder. paper. and fuse.

Like a ball that hits the rim as the clock runs out on a tied game, the sparkler sparked its last spark as it bounced and then fell into the box of My Precious.

But, as any child with a hand burn on the 5th of July knows, a sparker's stem stays red-hot for a half-life, and this suicide-machine of a sparkler nailed its landing upon the fuse of a Ground Bloom Flower.

I heard the *sssssss* of the fuse as it turned into flame.

My utter panic at that sound took over the deep freeze that had gripped me, and I rushed toward my box of Never-ending Happiness, much the way a pet owner would rush back into a house on fire to save their dog.

I heard the slow motion "NOOOOOOOO!!!!!!" in my ears before the truth hit me: It was my own voice.

And I was too late. As I neared the box, the Ground Bloom Flower did what Ground Bloom Flowers do.

It shot a pink flame out of its dragon-like mouth, and began a wild spin with a "Bzzzzzzzzzzt!!!!!" sound that I still hear on nights when I cannot sleep.

That pink flame danced and leapt from fuse to fuse in the box, to light the whole spreadsheet/meal/pyrotechnic opera at once.

The hiss of a hundred or more lit fuses bounced off the church building, the buildings across the street, and maybe the moon.

Then the fiery fuses touched the magic powder inside the tube of childhood wonder . . . and in the space of 0.00001 milliseconds set off each every one that was left.

The fireworks show each night at Disneyland could not compare to what we saw next.

Not the launch of a Space Shuttle or the Meteor that killed the dinosaurs could hold a Roman Candle to the grand show that shot from two square feet of cardboard.

I've seen a real volcano as its lava poured out. At night.

No way was it on a par with this.

Maybe an "Earthrise" from the ISS could come close, but there is no sound in space.

This had Sound. All The Sounds.

Fireworks that go bang and fireworks that shoot into the sky and fireworks that emit a burst of sparks and fireworks that do all of that — did do all of that.

All at once.

I could see the image of the lights bouncing off Mission Peak.

The Modesto Fire Department sent out a truck.

Area 51 called to ask if we had "something" that should belong to them.

My Dad, who had started to walk away, turned, and with crazed glee, hopped up and down, clapping and "Yippee'ing."

I'd never seen him do a thing like that.

But then he had never seen a thing like this.

And he'd fired artillery in the Army.

After about a minute, the early sunrise that had sprung from my Box of Broken Hopes and Dreams began to dim, and the mushroom cloud of smoke began to drift with the wind — some say to start the next cycle of Global Warming.

With the peal of the final Piccolo Pete came the rush of utter quiet.

That is, all that could be heard were the claps and whoops of my Dad.

My friends stood around me with no words. They knew and felt my great loss. As some — but not me — might put it. my *joie de vivre* had taken a major hit.

The Unnamed One, however, hung back from our group.

My Dad summed it up: "They usually do the finale at the end . . . be safe, kids." And he turned to head home.

My pals went back to their boxes of fireworks, with painstaking care moved them away from the trees, and then began the show that had shot out of my grasp that year.

I've had many Fourth Of July parties prior and since.

The memories of those are vague and with no order.

But this one — this ONE — is ever printed on my mind.

Had it not been for the errant Super Sparkler of Doom, that night would have just been one more vague memory.

But, in this case, it has been a lifelong memory and a touchstone to my youth.

In spite of how I felt about it at the time, to me it is part of what makes America like no other country on earth.

And we all know that the real Independence Day means a lot more than fireworks and hot dogs.

~ 5 ~
If You Can Keep It

Joanne Fleck

When Benjamin Franklin came out of the Constitutional Convention on September 18, 1787 a woman asked, "What have we got — a republic or a monarchy?" Franklin's reply was, "A republic, if you can keep it." As a child, I was proud to place my hand on my heart and say the pledge to our flag at school every day, with no thought of just how easy it would be to one day wake up and find our form of rule gone.

What can we do to keep this form of rule that we love so much? First, those who live in this land must learn how it works. I was taught how the three arms of our government — the body we elect to write our laws, the courts, and the man or woman we elect to serve in the White House — are meant to keep the power in check. Those who wrote the plan wished to have schools so that those who live in our land could learn to read and then could read the Constitution on their own.

It is for us to strive to bring back that goal.

Thus taught, each of us will be able and eager to voice our thoughts. The most basic way to do this is to use the right to vote. But we don't just vote in a void. We first take time to find out all we can about each man, and woman, and issue up for a vote and make sure each choice we make is well thought out. Then, when we see an issue that seems to need our input; we will be willing to take time to meet with, call, or write those in power.

Recently I sent an email to Representative about an issue that was on the House floor for a vote and also to a TV news show that I felt did not cover a topic well. I look up to those who have gone to the school boards to voice their worry over what is done in schools. We failed to ask our Congress to cut funds to colleges that let Marxists teach in them. That has come back to haunt us.

When my own city voted down a "light rail" line to add to our buses we did not raise our voice when they built it anyway. They used federal funds to cover most of the cost so they could get around our "no" vote. Since then, they have added some other light rail lines which came at a high cost in not only money but more crime. Only one of those lines was put to a vote and got a nod from the city. Not using our voice when we should does not end well. As Thomas Jefferson was thought to have said, "The price of freedom is eternal vigilance."

So that we can keep a republic, we strive to be moral. Evil rears its ugly head when a judge is bribed, when a cop uses force for the wrong cause, or when a vote count is changed. These kinds of things decay our form of rule.

John Adams wrote, "Our constitution was made only for a moral and religious people. It is wholly inadequate for the government of any other." So these days we pray that those who have turned away from God will turn toward Him. God can change hearts to be in tune with His heart. If we are "one nation, under God," we will be "indivisible, with liberty and justice for all." Once we are back to being truly "under God," I will have the same trust that I had as a child when I held my hand over my heart and said the pledge to our flag.

~ 6 ~
Home of the American Brave in England

Pamela Cosel

"Oh Beautiful for spacious skies, for amber waves of grain, for purple mountain majesties above the fruited plain." ("America the Beautiful," Kathryn Lee Bates, 1895)

As the morning sun rose behind dark rain clouds over the British Isles, the fact that it was Independence Day at home was on the minds of most members of the Greeley Chroale and as we continued our two-week singing tour of Scotland and England in the summer of 1996.

England has spacious skies and amber waves of grain.

But no purple mountains.

Red, white and blue colors fill flower boxes, line stone walks, and drape near wood gates. They shine bright beauty under the rainy, billowy clouds.

Americans blaze these colors on their flags.

* * *

"When Johnny comes marching home again, Hurrah, hurrah!" ("When Johnny Comes Marching Home" by Patrick Gilmore, 1863).

"First to fight for right and freedom . . ." (*Marines' Hymn,* author unknown*)*

On the British calendar the fourth of July is flanked on each side by the third and the fifth, as mute and stoic as a line of trained soldiers.

The day is just like any other to the English, our cousins across the sea, who live amid Cambridge academia where great kings and greater minds made some of the greatest discoveries we hold true today.

Here, the apple fell on Sir Isaac Newton's head, and scientists for the first time discussed DNA over lunch at "The Eagle," a local pub where beer has been served since the 1300s when the Saxons took over England . . . at least according to a local tour guide. Today, an American can view names scrawled on the ceiling by American soldiers posted in England during World War II. "The Wild Hair–9th Squadron" and "Bert's Boys–196th Squadron" left their marks.

* * *

"Oh, say can you see by the dawn's early light . . ." (*The Star-Spangled Banner* by Francis Scott Key*)*

As the morning sun rose from rain clouds that dripped over this North Sea isle country, Independence Day at home was on the minds of most of us in the Greeley Chorale as we went on with our two-week singing tour of Scotland and England.

Independence Day dawned seven hours ahead of Colorado and our friends and families back home. While those at home still slept, prior to the parades and pancake breakfasts, before barbecues began to smoke and children urged parents to light spitting Roman candles, we singers gave thought to being away from home on this of all holidays.

Many of us awoke in the homes of host families, Cambridge residents who housed half of the group for two nights. They met us with open arms and home-cooked meals, showed up at our concert, and shared many a story late into the night about their families and lives there.

Watch an English family for a short two days and you may find that the family unit in that country is more traditional — the parents very involved with their children — than families in the United States often are. But we also saw many ways that families are the same on both sides of the Atlantic: older sisters argue with younger brothers, teenagers like to spend time with their friends. Parents' busy work schedules along with children's school hours can make life hectic.

It turned out that, while many of the families were native Englishmen, some were from other countries, including the United States.

We singers spent the A.M. seeing the sights of Cambridge. We visited its grand halls of education and holy chapels, many of which date back to the time of 14th century kings. Our schooldays history texts came back to us as we read family charts of Kings Henry VI, VII and VIII — the latter of wife-beheading fame, his statue set high above the streets at many sites in King's College.

During summer break, students from around the world go to Cambridge to study the proper use of the English language.

* * *

"What so proudly we hailed at the twilight's last gleaming" (*The Star-Spangled Banner*).

With stars still aglow in the Colorado sky, it was mid-morning in England on the Fourth of July. It seemed an ordinary day other than the fact that nearly 100 of us were across the ocean, far away from the Fourth of July we knew. "What should we do?" we asked each other. We'd planned to sing patriotic songs at our evening concert: "An American Hymn" and "Give Me Your Tired, Your Poor." But could each of us honor that day in any other way that would make it feel like home, even though we were away?

* * *

"And the rockets' red glare . . ." (*The Star-Spangled Banner*)

We were on an adventure! A group of only 10, we jumped on a duel-deck tour bus to explore the local sights. With no firm plan in mind, we were led more by the guide than our spirits, as we sank into our seats. As it left the city, the bus sped past open green fields in the clear, sunny air.

It wasn't until the woman with the crisp British accent shared details about our first stop that red flags went up in my mind's eye — unfurled red, white, and blue — and there in the countryside, suddenly bands began to play in my head. We were at the Cambridge American Cemetery. Out of the blue, we had been given a chance to honor our Fourth of July.

* * *

"The bombs bursting in air…" (*The Star-Spangled Banner*)

Stretched below us on the hill's side were perfect rows of white crosses to mark graves of American servicemen and servicewomen. After the end of World War II, Cambridge University gave the United States this prime land in order to bury its brave soldiers who lost their lives in the fight to rid the world of the worst enemy it had ever seen.

A framed letter from President Dwight D. Eisenhower that thanked the future Queen Elizabeth and one from her in reply are on view in the cemetery's reception building. Those who visit can sign a guest book and leave a note for those who come later. A 3-ring binder holds photographs of other American cemeteries located in countries around the world.

The last page of the book tells the heroic story of a soldier, John Valdez, Jr., who was awarded the U.S. Medal of Honor for his brave actions, which led to the loss of his right foot. His plane went down while he was on his way home.

* * *

"…gave proof through the night that our flag was still there" (*The Star-Spangled Banner*).

At the entrance to the grounds, an 82-foot-high flagpole stands as a gift in honor of Joseph P. Kennedy, Jr., the eldest child of Joseph, Sr. and Ethel Kennedy. Nearby on the white stone wall, along with the names of all who are buried there, Valdez's name is etched in gold.

This towering wall runs from the entry side along a rectangular pond overflowing with white and red roses amid greenery built to reach just short of the steps of the memorial chapel located at the opposite end. Along the wall are larger-than-life-size carved statues of men in soldiers' uniforms, one for each branch of the American military services.

Inside the chapel, clear window panels to the north overlook the graves, bearing in their centers full-color engraved seals of each state in our union, while the south wall shows small images of each major event in WWII. The display portrays the strategic attack paths the American planes and ships followed as they closed in on enemy territory in Germany to end the war.

* * *

We had stood aside in a quiet group with one last view of the total scene in that place, a gift we had no prior idea about. Then, with somber thoughts of the sacrifices, we honored the dead who had given their lives.

We 10 stood, hands on our hearts, at the base of the flagpole in a foreign land and sang in clear, strong voices: "Oh, say, does that star-spangled banner yet wave — o'er the land of the free, and the home of the brave?" (*The Star-Spangled Banner*)

When Johnny Comes Marching Home
Patrick Gilmore

When Johnny comes marching home again
Hurrah, hurrah!
We'll give him a hearty welcome then,
Hurrah, hurrah!
The men will cheer, the boys will shout,
The ladies, they will all turn out,
And we'll all feel gay,
When Johnny comes marching home.

The old church bell will peal with joy,
Hurrah, hurrah!
To welcome home our darling boy,
Hurrah, hurrah!
The village lads and lassies say,
With roses, they will strew the way,
And we'll all feel gay,
When Johnny comes marching home.

Get ready for the jubilee,
Hurrah, hurrah!
We'll give the hero three times three,
Hurrah, hurrah!
The laurel wreath is ready now,
To place upon his loyal brow,
And we'll all feel gay,
When Johnny comes marching home.

Let love and friendship on that day,
Hurrah, hurrah!
Their choicest treasures then display,
Hurrah, hurrah!
And let each one perform some part,
To fill with joy the warrior's heart,
And we'll all feel gay,
When Johnny comes marching home.

~ 7 ~
No Land?

Lillian Joyce

At the age of eight, I looked out the clear round glass of the plane. Below me, the trees began to shrink into toy-sized plants. My trip had begun. For my father's time off from work, my family and I were on our way to the land my parents loved: America. I didn't share their sense of warmth.

On the next July 4th, I had worn a red shirt with a white-and-blue skirt but only out of duty. All the while, I thought of the time when I had worn green clothes for the Saudi Arabia national day. Which side should I stick with — the place where I grew up or the place my parents chose to call home?

In the leaves of my small blue book were many stamps from the areas I had flown to. On the last leaf, words of great weight walked in a straight line.

Name: Lillian Joyce

Nationality: United States of America.

Those words were proof. I must wear red, white, and blue.

While on the way to the watch shop with my grandma, I saw a strange sign. The short sides had curves like up-side-down bumps.

"What is that?" I asked.

"You don't know? Of course, you didn't grow up here. You wouldn't know."

With that, my wish to know fled. My mind stayed blank as Grandma said, "The sign says the movie theater is ahead."

Deep down in my heart where I could not see or hear them, words tried to fight back. *I am not dumb. Do you know what Halawa is? Do you know how to wear a hijab?*

So then I was sure that my nationality was not proof of who I was. In fact, it was what I knew about a land's facts that proved who I was so it was right for me to wear a green shirt. I must be Arab.

In my mind, I went back years to a mall in Saudi Arabia where my mother and I had gone to shop for food. The noise of strange words I couldn't yet grasp met my ears. Young girls stared at me as they stood next to their mothers — dressed in black Abayas. In their eyes, I was still the white American girl.

The thought of that time told me I could not wear green. Even in Saudi Arabia, I didn't fit in. I changed the place I called my own once again. I couldn't make the right choice. Each one I tried was wrong.

As I passed my teen years and found a job, I let all the colors fall away. I chose black — not a color of one nationality over the other. I lived as a guest in each land.

When asked, "What is Saudi Arabia's national dish?" I said, "I don't know; ask an Arab."

When asked, "What do Americans like to eat?" I said, "I don't know, ask an American."

At last, I could rest in peace. I didn't fight each week about which side I fit in.

While at work, I was sent a card. It said, "Come to my house at 12:00 PM. Bring a dish from your nationality." At 12:15 I walked into the house. Folks had brought plates filled with food from the Netherlands, Benin, Italy, Germany and America. But not me. In my hands was a plate full of fruit.

"I love all these new foods! Did you try the German food I made? What type of food did you make, Lillian? Where is it from?"

"The store."

The German left.

It isn't my fault. I had no choice. It was the way I was raised. I have no land that I can claim.

At the start of a new life in a new land, I sat on a couch. A new friend sat on a chair beside me.

"It doesn't make sense," said I.

"Yes, it does. You grew up in more than one land."

"But I can't be one or the other. I don't know either place. Each nationality I pick is wrong."

"Lillian, there is no right or wrong. You can be American or Arab or a mix of the two on any day that you wish. Red, white, blue, and green — each one of them is a part of who you are."

At the age of 25, I watched the toy-like trees from the clear glass of the plane. Inch by inch, the trees began to grow in size. The plane's wheels bounced on the ground. The trip had come to an end. As I walked down the steps; red, blue, white, green, yellow, purple, and pink held up a sign: "Welcome Home!"

~ 8 ~
A Call to Act

Alice H. Murray

Many think of patriotism in terms of what they feel. They love and take pride in the U.S.A. and wish to honor it. But they may feel patriotic only now and then such as on Independence Day or when they hear "The Star-Spangled Banner." Yet patriotism is so much more than what we feel. It spurs us to act.

How do we act to show patriotism? It could be a small thing such as being still and quiet with your hand over heart at the sound of "The Star-Spangled Banner." Or it may be a citizen who flies his flag on his house for all to see.

True patriotism leads to more than these simple acts, which don't call for much work from a citizen. It leads us to give of our time for the good of this country. Uncle Sam truly wants YOU!

If we love our land, we want the best for it, not only today but in the days ahead. We can shape what is to occur when we vote. That does not mean just going to the poll and being a warm body who puts X's on the ballot. It means to take the time to learn about those who want to hold office and how they stand on each issue. It also means being up on what is going on in the land and what the one who holds office would face and deal with.

As a child, I saw my parents vote every time they had the chance. Now that I'm grown, I, like them, vote in every election. From the time they were very small, I would take my kids to the polls with me so they could learn about what they would do as an adult. I care about the U.S.A. and to me, it is an honor to vote. I have even taken a class to work at the polls on Election Day so folks can vote. I honor my country by the gift of my time in doing this work.

Some feel a duty to the U.S.A and act to serve in the military. That role costs them time away from their loved ones and is a risk to their very lives. But their job makes the U.S.A. strong and helps to keep it free. Honor shines bright in what they do for love of country.

Not all will be in the military. But each of us can pray for those who serve to be safe. We can thank active-duty military for what they do for us, and the U.S.A. We can ease their minds when we help their loved ones back home while they are gone. My daughter's husband was in the U.S. Army and spent weeks in a far land where his life was in peril. His being away took a toll on both him and his family, but he rose to the task out of a deep sense of patriotism.

If we care for our country, we can pray for those who lead it, and ask God to help them in their roles. They need Him to point them toward the wise way to go.

An old adage tells us "actions speak louder than words." That idea is true with patriotism. We can say we love our country and want to honor it. But are words about how we feel about the U.S.A. all we offer? True patriotism calls for more. It calls upon us to act. So we fly our flag. We sing "The Star-Spangled Banner."

We learn what is going on in our country. We vote on Election Day. Some of us enter the military or help those who have. But most of all, we pray for our country. God bless America!

~ 9 ~
Look Past World War II

Carol Baird

May the God of hope fill you with all joy

Romans 15:13 NKJV

One still night, in a dark room, fear filled the air. A gun lay on Dad's lap. Mom held Dad's hand as they sat on the side of the bed. Mom shook in fear. As a small child of five or six, I sat arm in arm with her. Mom and Dad were filled with a faith that took them out of their fear, but in my eyes, fear was in every breath I took.

As we looked out of the dull glass pane, all we saw came from porch lights on a few homes just down the block. We sat and stared at the empty street. There was a sound. Clack, clack, clack, clack, and then the noise came to a stop. A girl cried out in a shrill scream.

Men who were mere boys of draft age had been called up to serve in a world war, but some men dodged the draft. A few girls signed on to fight the war in air or on soil where they met with bombs that burst in their sight. Wives were left in charge of the home. Young girls took jobs in the mills, drove trucks, or joined the Red Cross as they sought to do their part to serve at home.

With no phone to call for help, fright fell on the girls from the threat of harm by men who prowled at night. These wolves walked through the town and trolled back and forth on the street. Their aim was to find a crawl space next to a door. There they'd wait in the dark, like a cat at night, set to pounce on their prey. The gal who came home late or the one who set out for the third shift at the mill was fresh game.

It fell to men at home, such as my dad, to be the shield and guard. He was a stay-at-home dad whose goal was to keep peace — a good man who knew the risks of wrong that might be done if no one cared. Dad didn't go off to war. He was kept home to serve in a key role on army tanks in the mill. He was on watch for those who prowled at night.

Though times like this in the World War II years were seen through my child's eyes and ears, they formed for the most part from Mom and Dad's view. My young mind knew what I saw and heard in the dark. Fear came when I heard tales of war. The brief life I had known before had changed.

Fear shapes a heart, but we act with the brain. Lack of food in the 1940s made us store more, use food stamps, and save S&H green stamps. Mom and Dad bought war bonds to help fund the war. Even after the war, their mind-set didn't end. I learned to hoard more than I would use and not share what I should.

War also changed fun for us kids. Mom and I played a new card game named "War." The boys and girls on my street played war with toy guns, caps that pop, and play knives. Spy and war films were shown at our town hall.

Two boys, Wayne aged 14 and his 12-year-old brother Glen, filled carts with tin cans, iron and steel scraps, and their mom's pots and pans. They wheeled the cart to a yard that bought junk for cash. The mills bought up the scrap to make parts for planes.

My mom urged me to pray and give thanks for those who put their lives on the front line of fire. But I thought I should give thanks for those who stayed and worked in my town. Mom and Dad's friends didn't shed their blood, but they did offer up their sweat to help the war. They paid a high toll as each worked hard to do their part to keep us safe. If you were to walk the streets in this small town, you would see one or more stars on each door. Each star stood for a loved one who had died in the war — one a day that brought tears and a vast change to those who grieved. The fear of loss lay at the back of each one's mind.

Now grown, I look past my fear in World War II to see what America meant to me at war's end, and every day since.

In school, I stood, placed my hand on my heart, and pledged to the flag of the United States of America. Each boy and girl in the room knew they were free to bow their heads in prayer and to sit at their desks and read God's Word.

I was proud to raise my voice and sing, "O say can you see by the dawn's early light . . . ." — the piece Francis Scott Key wrote that was now America's national anthem. These words say we are a land of the free and the home of the brave. This song spells out hope for me in a land that stands for all that is right.

Each one who gave their best in a world war where they stood up for the right to be free paid the cost. I now cheer and give thanks from a heart filled with love, joy, peace, and hope in God who gave up His own son to die to make us free.

America was formed by men of faith in God, men who sought to build a home where all could be free.

"America, America, God shed His grace on thee."

~ 10 ~
A Young Land Put to the Test

Russell MacClaren

On September 15, 1814, the U.S. faced a major power that had just beat Napolean and was forcing its will on all other nations. The young, newly-formed country fought an empire with superior numbers of ships, guns, and men.

The British had marched toward the White House, which caused President Madison and his wife, Dolley, to flee while British troops torched Washington D.C. Thanks to Mrs. Madison, state papers and the Gilbert Stuart image of George Washington were saved.

From Washington, the English marched on Baltimore, the third largest city in the United States. American pirates docked at its port, the second largest after New York. Only Fort McHenry, under Major Armistead — with 1,000 men and a few cannon in poor shape — stood between the British and the town. British ships under Admiral Cochrane sailed into the port, but wrecked ships blocked the harbor. So from far away, the English trained their guns on the walls of Fort McHenry. The Americans fought 5,000 ground troops and guns from the British fleet, but with the death of British Major General Robert Ross and a timely storm, the American fort held; and Admiral Cochrane sailed off.

On that night, through the siege, Fort McHenry glowed with bursts of bombs and fire every minute. As day broke, the Americans took down their storm flag and raised a banner so large it could be seen for miles.

All the while, from an American ship in the harbor where he was under guard* Francis Scott Key, a young lawyer, watched the fight in fear for his country. When he saw the sign that the Fort McHenry force had won, he penned the words that millions of loyal Americans have joined to sing down through the ages.

*To keep him safe until he could negotiate with the British fleet to release a Baltimore citizen who had been taken prisoner.

The Star-Spangled Banner
by Francis Scott Key

O say can you see, by the dawn's early light,
What so proudly we hail'd at the twilight's last gleaming,
Whose broad stripes and bright stars through the perilous fight
O'er the ramparts we watch'd were so gallantly streaming?
And the rocket's red glare, the bombs bursting in air,
Gave proof through the night that our flag was still there,
O say does that star-spangled banner yet wave
O'er the land of the free and the home of the brave?

On the shore dimly seen through the mists of the deep
Where the foe's haughty host in dread silence reposes,
What is that which the breeze, o'er the towering steep,
As it fitfully blows, half conceals, half discloses?
Now it catches the gleam of the morning's first beam,
In full glory reflected now shines in the stream,
'Tis the star-spangled banner - O long may it wave
O'er the land of the free and the home of the brave!

And where is that band who so vauntingly swore,
That the havoc of war and the battle's confusion
A home and a Country should leave us no more?
Their blood has wash'd out their foul footstep's pollution.

No refuge could save the hireling and slave
From the terror of flight or the gloom of the grave,
And the star-spangled banner in triumph doth wave
O'er the land of the free and the home of the brave.

O thus be it ever when freemen shall stand
Between their lov'd home and the war's desolation!
Blest with vict'ry and peace may the heav'n rescued land
Praise the power that hath made and preserv'd us a nation!
Then conquer we must, when our cause it is just,
And this be our motto - "In God is our trust,"
And the star-spangled banner in triumph shall wave
O'er the land of the free and the home of the brave.

~ 11 ~
Why I Fly the Flag

Desiree St. Clair Spears

Every year on June 14th, I hang my flag. I was born on that date, but that's not why I fly the flag. June 14th is also Flag Day, but that's not the main cause of why I do this. The family of the poet who wrote "The Star-Spangled Banner" once owned the farm on which I live, yet that's not why I fly the flag.

But I do take Key's words "O say, can you see . . ." to heart.

As I hang my the flag, I see each color and think about what it means to me: red for the blood shed; white, a young nation; and blue, one that is just, alert, and works hard. I watch the stripes wave in the wind and the sun shine through the stars. I think of those who sailed the seas for a fresh start, a chance to worship as they saw fit. Most of all, I think of those who came to the shores of Maryland to start a colony, only a few miles from my home on the farm. Two of them were my 7th great-grandparents, and I give thanks for their brave souls.

Just past the flag, I see the waves of grain in the field that lines my yard. I think of those who were here first, who lived and died on this very land where I now stand, who learned to live side by side with the white man and taught him how to grow crops. I give honor to them.

I think of my father and grandfather, my uncles and cousins, who worked this land, too. They grew crops, raised hens, and milked cows to feed their family. I give thanks for them, for the chance to live off this land — and the chance to live on it.

Past the field is the house where I grew up. Where I learned how to live and how to love. Where I played and where I worked. Where I felt safe. And where I knelt to pray. And it was there in my room on the top floor where I strummed my guitar and sang, "This land is your land, this land is my land." I was glad to have my own place.

I give thanks for the value of hard work, which I learned on the farm and at school. I give thanks for my teachers who taught me more than math, such as how to read and play guitar. I am glad I was able to go to school and later to give back — to teach for 20 years.

I give thanks for being able to raise my children (as a solo mom) on the same farm, to send them to the same school (for free), and to teach them to pray. And when money was short, how we all prayed! Not only did we get help from family and our church, but also from our state. I am blessed by a country that helps those in need.

Now I share this home on the farm with my new husband, who is a Coast Guard vet. His father was an Army war vet, and now his son serves in the Army. I am proud to be part of a family who serves and of a country that takes a stand for what is right. I give thanks for all the men and women who have served and now serve to guard this land, its shores, and all of us.

After World War II, my husband's father, an African American, met and wed a German woman, my husband's mother.

Oh how I give thanks for their love, which has given me mine! And I give thanks for a country where folks of every race, tribe, or tongue can come and live — or learn to live — side by side.

Now at 63 and blessed that I don't have to work, I have more time to think and pray — to sit on my porch and take in the view. I look over the fields of gold, lift my eyes to the skies with no end, and spot an eagle in flight. In awe, I watch it soar from east to west. My heart swells, and my mouth fills with praise for the One who made all of this "America the Beautiful."

Of course I know that America is not right all the time, but there is a lot right about her. And that's why I fly the flag.

O say, can you see?

~ 12 ~

What 9/11 Taught Me About My Country

Beverly Robertson

As a child, I felt safe in our land. Two cousins served in Vietnam, and I wrote to them and prayed for them a few times. Years went by, and not until 9/11 did I think our home land was at risk. But this day changed all that. On a bright, clear morn, I went to work as an aide in a school. I had just left a class, when in the hall I heard a hushed voice say that a plane had hit one of the twin towers in New York. In a while, the one next to it was hit by plane #2. I wasn't sure if this was the day my daughter, Terry, was set to work in the city; but I thought she had gone in that day. She was in her eighth month. I hadn't heard any more news so went home at noon to see if Terry or her husband, Michael, had called. They hadn't, but calls came in from Michael's folks. They had not heard from them and thought it could be a bomb that harms one's cell phones.

What I saw on the TV shocked me. Dark rolls of smoke streamed by on the screen. I knew Michael worked next to the towers. This part of the Big Apple was on fire. Folks ran for their lives, and brave men rushed to save them.

I went back to school to help keep our kids calm.

At last, we heard from Terry and Michael. Terry told us that she had seen folks toss off their shoes so they could run with more speed. Some were cloaked in ash and store clerks gave them clothes and shoes for quick cash. New Yorkers stopped to care for each other, which is not what they're known for.

As for Michael, he had rushed to find Terry at work and was so upset that he went to the wrong store. She had moved to a new site, and he had gone to the old one. Her boss was still there and gave him a ride to the right location.

Then Terry and Michael had to find a new route to pick up their daughter at a child care in New Jersey. They first left New York by the subway. Then they moved to a PATH train and had to take three trains in all. In New Jersey, they got on a bus. When it reached the end of the line, they had to plod on with sore feet. Their fears eased as they saw that the man and his wife from next door had come to pick them up. When they saw their daughter, they stepped up their pace to a trot and smiles spread on each face. The wife had gone to get their child. How glad they were to see and kiss their babe and after that give thanks to the woman who had brought her to them!

What joy to find our loved ones all safe and back at home! In my heart I once again vowed to give thanks to God for those we love — every day from that day on. I also vowed to pray for the land I love so much and do all I can to keep it free.

~ 13 ~
They Show Us What a Patriot Is

Judson I. Stone

My parents taught my brothers and me to place worth on historic sites, museums, and national parks. We visited these places when we moved from one Air Force Base to the next one. I saw how big, beautiful, and diverse our country is. My wife and I have done the same thing for our sons.

Love for country and family are big parts of being a patriot. I have patriotic thoughts and feelings, but I don't call myself a patriot. I save that name for those who served in war. My dad and son each served in two wars. Dad was a pilot in World War II and a surgeon in Vietnam.

After dad left home for Vietnam, I wrote a poem about how I missed him. The poem, *Gone Is He*, ends with the goal I hoped for:

Gone is he to a far-off place.
Gone is he to a war-torn place.
Gone is he to the sun's resting place.
He is kept from the wanted rest.
He will be gone for twelve full moons.
Gone is he from us, but he is in
The minds of people today.

> Gone from his country but helping another.
> He will be back but gone is he.

With a high draft number in 1970, I did not fear a call up, and I did not choose to volunteer the way my dad or son did. I have served my country in other ways when I vote, write letters to share my views, and give of my time in towns where I have lived.

In 2005, my son Nathaniel joined the Army and went to boot camp. His mother and I prayed. I wrote to him to make sure he knew the costs for him to join. He would lose liberties and could be harmed or killed. But he stayed true to the choice to face threat for his country. For his mom's part — she mailed care boxes for him and his fellow soldiers. She also called for prayer warriors to join her in prayers.

In July of 2006, Nathaniel left boot camp to say goodbye to us and to his friends who came over to our house. We ate good food and watched *End of the Spear*. We spoke the best we could about our love, pride, and aid for him. We shed tears and prayed with him.

In late August, I visited Nathaniel in hot and humid Louisiana at Fort Polk, where he trained with his unit. His weekend pass gave us two days. We bowled three games, and I lost them all. The 2006 movie *Invincible* about Vince Papale who made the Philadelphia Eagles' team charmed us. It tells a good father-son tale that brought tears to my eyes, even though their tale was not ours.

Sunday worship helped us think of God and pray. As we shared a last meal with each other, I found courage to speak of my love and my fears and how proud I was of him. While I talked, Nathaniel kept quiet. He had steeled himself for war. It wasn't until three days after I left, that I was able to see what he had thought about my words when, in an email to family and friends, he shared what I had said to him.

On the way home from Fort Polk back home to Arlington, Texas, I called his high-school football coach who had served with the Marines. He said, "Tell him to keep his head down." I did just that. His unit flew back to Fort Richardson, Alaska, and then, a few weeks later, shipped off to war in Iraq.

Four months later early on a Sunday when my parents, a brother and sister-in-law, our youngest son, and my wife and I were about to leave our house for church, the phone rang. We heard our son's voice. He spoke from a hospital in Iraq. He told us that an Improvised Explosive Device (IED) had hit his Humvee under the engine. Nathaniel and his three friends had all shed blood but were still alive. They had gone back to their post to heal. When the okay came, they went back to join the fray and served until the end of their tour nine months later.

That Sunday my wife had been set to sing and I to preach in our church's evening service. We were in shock and talked about backing out of our roles, but in the end chose to stay with the plan. Jan found it hard to smile as she sang. I preached about the death of Ezekiel's wife (Ezekiel 24:15-27). The worst that could take place for her did, but the worst for us — a mom and dad — did not. The war did not take our son. We praise God that he lived through it.

I honor my son's war service, and thank him every chance I get. I also love to thank other vets. Many were called up for a war that changed their life plans. Others chose to go to war.

All of these show us what a patriot is. To me, their heroism is no less grand than the Grand Tetons that my parents took my brothers and me to see when we moved from South Carolina to California, and I view it with the same awe. Ours is a big, beautiful, and diverse country that I cherish. Men and women have fought to guard our great land and the truths we hold so dear. These are the true patriots.

~ 14 ~
Liberty Sleeps

Jennifer Cotney

She's not yet dead! Her pulse still beats,
Her lungs still draw deep breaths.
Though, I do agree, she seems so weak,
It's too soon to plan her death.

She's got good bones — under skin that sags,
She's worn and shows her age.
It's been some time since she last shined,
But we all know how looks fade.

She's slow to speak; her tone is mute,
Drowned out by other noise,
And no one cares to hear from her
When she dares to lift her voice.

If you look at her with just your eyes,
You'd think the end is near.
And those who wait to watch her die
Bet it will be this year.

But don't be fooled by her weak state
And don't yet count her out.
As long as blood pumps through her veins,
It'll be hard to take her down.

All of us need time to rest,
A blessed time to heal.
And as long as she can draw a breath,
God could use her still.

She's got more nerve than it seems
And twice as much of hope.
She's known to be the queen of dreams
And there's fire in her soul.

It's true, she needs a lot of work
But she's got the will to try.
And as we all pray for her,
She'll find the strength to fight.

So while liberty sleeps, pray with me
That our nation turns back to God.
For America is not yet dead! Her heart still beats!
And blessed hope still reigns.

~ 15 ~
Glad to Devote My Life

Eddie Burchfield

In 1950, I was born in Bessemer, Alabama, to parents who were both WWII veterans. My dad, Edward, a Sergeant in the 12th Calvary Division, served in the Pacific Conflict. My mother, Margaret, was a Corporal in the Army Air Corp (WAC); her job was to pack parachutes. Patriotism was not so much talked about in our house; it just *was*.

Every day American children would play army, watch military shows, say the Pledge of Allegiance, and pray in school. The awe my family had for the American flag and all it stood for was above all else. As I grew up in the 60s, I, too, began to be aware of not only how truly great America is but also that the world of that time was a place full of threat.

Vietnam was a new war and in the news every day. The "conflict" seemed to hit home with all of us and caused America to split apart. Half of America was as patriotic as ever, but the other half was anti-war and marched in the streets.

Right after I graduated from Bessemer Technical School in 1971, I received my draft notice from the United States Army. Sent to Fort Polk, Louisiana, for basic training, I was schooled in Infantry to be sent to Vietnam. I went on to serve two years active duty and seven years in the Army Guard.

As it worked out, I was never sent to Vietnam, but I served in several states and two countries — once in Japan, and twice in South Korea. In my nine years of service, I have four MOS's (Military Occupational Specialties): as a Clerk-Typist, a Bass Player in the 55th Army Band at Redstone Arsenal (Huntsville, Alabama), a Multi-Channel Radio Operator in the 711 Signal Battalion (Mobile, Alabama), and my last 5 years as a Chaplains Assistant/Acting Chaplain in the same unit. Over those many years, I gained a deep respect for discipline and grew in my love for country.

I am proud to be an American, a veteran, and a Christian. I fly an American flag and still tear up when I hear the "The Star-Spangled Banner."

The United States of America is the best nation on earth. I love this land.

It all boils down to this: What patriotism means to me is that I have been glad to pledge years of my life and risk my death for our country.

"Hooah!"

The U.S. Air Force Song

Off we go into the wild blue yonder,
Climbing high into the sun;
Here they come zooming to meet our thunder,
At 'em now, Give 'em the gun! give em the gun!
Down we dive, spouting our flame from under,
Off with one helluva roar!
We live in fame or go down in flame. Hey!
Nothing'll stop the U.S. Air Force!

Brilliant minds fashioned a crate of thunder,
Sent it high into the blue;
Valiant hands blasted the world asunder;
How they lived God only knew!
Boundless souls dreaming of skies to conquer
Gave us wings, ever to soar!
With scouts before and bombers galore. Hey!
Nothing'll stop the U.S. Air Force!

Here's a toast to the host
Of those who love the vastness of the sky,
To a friend we send a message of the brave who serve on high.
We drink to those who gave their all of old
Then down we roar to score the rainbow's pot of gold.
A toast to the host of those we boast, the U.S. Air Force!

Off we go into the wild sky yonder,
Keep the wings level and true;
If you'd live to be a grey-haired wonder
Keep the nose out of the blue!
Fly to fight, guarding the nation's border,
We'll be there, followed by more!
In echelon we carry on.
Oh, nothing'll stop the U.S. Air Force![2]

~ 16 ~
Love of Country

Leah Hinton

Oxford Advanced Learner's Dictionary tells us patriotism is "love of your country and the desire to defend it." This brings to mind an army ready to fight, or laws meant to uphold what is right. As in many things, we tend lose sight of the small efforts that are more than flags on houses and fireworks on a summer night. They mean more than to just stand, hats off, for the Pledge of Allegiance.

My view on patriotism isn't the same as it is for many. One could say I look at it from an angle not seen by all — at least not these days. And that is okay, for I know that many do live with patriotism in their hearts, whether they know it or not.

My Grandpa, Billy Bob Harper, flew B-17s in World War II. He wasn't first in line to sign up, but he did so as soon as he was able, and he raised me to live with patriotism as part of my day-to-day life, even though I will never pilot a war bird. Yes, I vote. Yes, I speak up when those who make our laws need to hear my voice.

But to hold patriotism in our hearts daily is a whole other thing, the thing he learned only as a very young man going to war.

Grandpa Harper told me how his dad, Ray, was a grocer who, as part of his work during the war, took charge of his small

Kansas town's Victory Garden. Many people had their own Victory Gardens, but Ray's was meant for all. No one would go hungry in that rural town. My Grandpa's mom, Carrie, came up with recipes for when rations were tight so the children would have meals that not only fed their bodies but also fed their souls with hope and comfort. (This is a trait of hers I share – based on the truth that to feed people is to love them!) Grandpa's little brother, George, too young to sign up, held metal drives and rubber drives and in other ways did his best state-side to show his love of country. This was patriotism at its height. To me, these efforts were just as patriotic as the efforts of those sent half a world away to fight for liberty. Out of love, all hands were on deck to defend our nation and the collective American Dream it stands for.

But it is easy, isn't it, to feel the call to patriotism when we are under attack? I saw groups come together to pray when the Twin Towers came down. I've seen stars in windows on my block to tell of a son or daughter gone to fight. But when the plight of our military isn't front-page news, what do we do? In what way do we care for the pillars and ideals of this country? How do we show patriotism when no one's there to pull on the strings of our hearts?

Patriotism means more than to stand up for our country in war. Patriotism means to love and hold up our country day after day in the way we came together and the way we loved and stood up for each other.

Today we might not have a Victory garden, but we can surely feed our neighbor. We might not have rations, but whatever our means, we can ration what we have so that we can share with others. Each thing we do to create a rich life for each other stands guard for the American Dream. That Dream burns in our hearts. It is up to us to stoke the fire of that Dream while at the same time we keep in our minds that each of our families came to North America from a place on the other side of the seas and had to hold on to that dream until they became woven into the cloth our flag is made from. (My people come from Germany, England, and Sweden; yet are all now American.)

Some would argue that the image I paint here is more faith than patriotism. But the two work as one. The patriotism we hold guards our way of life and leaves us free to share that faith and live our ideals. When the two are split one from the other, we have crisis since both patriotism without faith and faith without love and respect for the land on which we pray can cause a nation to fall apart.

A nation's greatest resource is its people, and in the care of each other we show our greatest love of country. If a nation doesn't put the love of its people and for its people as the front line of patriotism, that nation will not last. So we fan the flames of patriotism in our hearts and know that the love we show those around us stands guard over the values, ideals, and love that makes our nation worth so much. We can wear our patriotism as a badge of love for each other.

Over There
by George M. Cohan (1917)

Johnnie get your gun, get your gun, get your gun,
Take it on the run, on the run, on the run;
Hear them calling you and me;
Every Son of Liberty.
Hurry right away, no delay, go today,
Make your Daddy glad, to have had such a lad,
Tell your sweetheart not to pine,
To be proud her boy's in line.

Chorus:
Over there, over there,
Send the word, send the word over there,
That the Yanks are coming, the Yanks are coming,
The drums rum-tumming everywhere.
So prepare, say a prayer,
Send the word, send the word to beware,
We'll be over, we're coming over,
And we won't come back till it's over over there.

Johnnie get your gun, get your gun, get your gun,
Johnnie show the Hun, you're a son-of-a-gun,
Hoist the flag and let her fly,
Like true heroes do or die.
Pack your little kit, show your grit, do your bit,
Soldiers to the ranks from the towns and the tanks,
Make your Mother proud of you,
And to liberty be true.

Chorus

~ 17 ~
A Flag, a Prayer, and a Journey Home

Penny L. Hunt

It was a fresh, crisp October day at our home in Quito, Ecuador. The phone rang, and I was surprised to hear my mother's voice.

"We have just learned that Dad is in his final hours," my mother said through tears.

"Oh no, Mom. It's too soon. What can I do?"

"The hospice nurse said you need to come now if you hope to have any time with him."

I was living high in the Andes, and my father was dying in Magnolia, Texas.

A last-minute flight was more than I could pay for. I rang my husband Bill at the embassy to see if he could help me get back to the USA. Calls were made, notes were sent, but no U.S. military planes were set to fly to Ecuador for weeks. I prayed and asked God for help.

Bill called back with the news that in three hours, a reserve-training unit from Kelly Air Force Base in San Antonio would be stopping for fuel in Ecuador. But that would be in Guayaquil — 300 miles away! *Can I get there in time?*

I soon found a hop that could get me to Guayaquil. After I set up care for the kids, I threw a change of clothes into a bag and ran to the Quito airport.

The flight was quick, and a waiting taxi took me to the military-landing strip. In the small, hot, waiting area, I saw a few cracked seats and some slow fans that stirred the smell of stale coffee and cigarettes.

I must have been an odd sight to the men there, alone with my red carry-on bag and straw hat. Wound tight as a ball of yarn, with as many loose ends to tie up, my head began to pound.

What if the plane doesn't come? Is Mom doing ok? What am I going to say to Dad? Will I even make it in time?

In what seemed like seconds, the room hummed with news that the C-130 cargo plane had landed. Through the window, its big, grey nose rolled into view . . . then its great wings . . . then a huge red, white, and blue American flag painted on its tail. I could not hold back the tears. My flag, my country, and my way home! My heart filled with thanks, I climbed the stairs and took my seat among the brave young men on that plane.

God had granted my plea; He'd brought me home for my father's final breath.

~ 18 ~

The Over-and-Above Patriot

Jasmine Gatti

We long for true citizenship, to pledge our wills along with those friends who fight for the same cause. Deep in our hearts we sense that "the truth will set [us] free" (John 8:32 ESV). In some way, we know this is real and good and patriotic — at least from man's point of view.

As is often the case, my earth-bound patriotism began in my family. But as I grew, this patriotism morphed *over and above* that into a sacred patriotism.

Eighty years ago in the 1940's, my parents fled war and fear in China. Ready to grab democracy, be free, and work hard for the American dream, they turned their backs on the life they had known — their lands, parents, homes, and jobs in Hong Kong, BCC, and Fukien on the south coast of China.

My mother, father, China-born siblings, and aunts drove from San Francisco to Washington, D.C. on Route 40. On this, their first road trip, they stopped in the Black Hills of South Dakota. I still have their black-and-white photo, taken below Mt. Rushmore. When I was a child it stood framed on our fridge, a sign to never look back. No more allegiance to an old land, only to the new American one. It was hard and it cost them. Many held tight to the song that rings out, "This land is your land; this land is my land from California to the New York Island . . . ." (*This Land Is Your Land* by Woody Guthrie).

My family's saga began over many seas and WWII fields of battle, full of risks and patriotic sacrifices like these:

It must have been hard when my dad fought the Japanese with their flag of the Rising Sun. He was part of the American Red Cross and risked being in the sights of friendly fire because he looked so much like the enemy.

It was hard for American soldiers not to get mixed up when the north and south Koreans were split apart from their union yet looked alike. All the while, my father fought in the same uniform and with the same goal and same blood that flowed red, white, and blue as the other U.S. GI's.

Years later at Da Nang, my brother faced the same threat from his own side — though in his army fatigues — when he fought in the Vietnam War. Who were the stealth good guys, who were the Viet Cong, and who were Asian-American fighters?

Off the battlefield, with more school and re-tooling, the family — out of great thanks — gave back to the U.S. as doctors and scientists. Three generations also worked in federal and state public health, park services, and U.S. diplomacy. Some of us in the Veterans' Administration cared for those with war wounds from PTSD, lost limbs, and lungs scarred by toxins.

Like other families and other Vets who do the same, they gave back. And they trusted in God to right the scales.

But the truth is that along with our patriotism on earth — all this will pass away with time. This is what I've learned in the time since I was a child who stared at that snapshot on the fridge.

When I join God, I'm a true citizen of His kingdom. When I see others and others see me from God's view, we all join in a pledge to our one King, one real president. His kingdom knows no end. It is vast and full. Our bonded hearts get to bow in true love and full freedom at the feet of our Lord Jesus Christ — not just a cause, a king, or a president on earth. To Him, we gladly sing praises of, "Glory, glory, hallelujah! His truth is marching on." This is why we know in depth that the truth that will set us free is Jesus. Let it sit in our hearts and make each of us an *over and above* patriot.

Battle Hymn of the Republic
by Julia Ward Howe

Mine eyes have seen the glory of the coming of the Lord
He is trampling out the vintage where the grapes of wrath
   are stored
He hath loosed the fateful lightning of His terrible swift sword
His truth is marching on

Glory, Glory, hallelujah!
Glory, glory, hallelujah!
Glory, glory, hallelujah!
His truth is marching on

I have seen Him in the watch-fires of a hundred circling camps
They have built Him an altar in the evening dews and damps
I can read His righteous sentence by the dim and flaring lamps
His day is marching on.

Glory, glory, hallelujah!
Glory, glory, hallelujah!
Glory, glory, hallelujah!
His day is marching on

I have read a fiery gospel writ in burnished rows of steel
"As ye deal with my contemners, so with you my grace shall deal"
Let the Hero, born of woman, crush the serpent with his heel
Since God is marching on

Glory, glory, hallelujah!
Glory, glory, hallelujah!
Glory, glory, hallelujah!
Since God is marching on

He has sounded forth the trumpet that shall never call retreat
He is sifting out the hearts of men before His judgment-seat
Oh, be swift, my soul, to answer Him! Be jubilant, my feet!
Our God is marching on

Glory, glory, hallelujah!
Glory, glory, hallelujah!
Glory, glory, hallelujah!
Our God is marching on

In the beauty of the lilies Christ was born across the sea
With a glory in His bosom that transfigures you and me
As He died to make men holy, let us die to make men free
While God is marching on

Glory, glory, hallelujah!
Glory, glory, hallelujah!
Glory, glory, hallelujah!
While God is marching on

~ 19 ~
Patriotic by Nature?

Pam Groves

In 1965, I added a Christmas card to the box of cards my high school was sending to soldiers in Vietnam. I didn't think of it as an act of patriotism. When I got back a letter from Charles R. Powers SP4 and then wrote back to him, patriotism was not in my thoughts. Months later when the box of home-baked cookies I had sent to him came back unopened marked on it one word "deceased," patriotism still didn't come to mind.

Decades later, when I said to a senior-aged man wearing a cap with a military insignia on it, "Thank you for your service," I did not know if he was in the military because of patriotism or the draft. When I wait in line to vote, I don't know if the people are there out of respect for our right to vote or in the hope that the bill to raise taxes fails. Does the school janitor I watch raising the flag in the school front yard do so with a patriotic heart or as one more chore for the day? I don't know.

I have taken part in planned acts of patriotism such as singing the national anthem with gusto at an event, waving the flag at a Veterans' Day Parade and putting up decor for Independence Day. I pay my taxes with as little fuss as possible. I have sent letters — both pro and con — to those who govern.

I have given my time to assist in our local school and on school-district committees. Taking part in these planned acts is taking part in patriotism.

Do patriotic acts occur when we aren't thinking about or planning them, yes! In looking back at my life, I recall seeing many family members and friends doing such acts. Not long ago my young grandson asked me, "Why did you say, 'thank you for your service' to that man?'" His words — and the very fact that he asked them — gave me pause. I, too, can pass on the keys to patriotism.

That is a power we all have.

~ 20 ~
The Capitol Remains

Jeff Brady

ELECTION DAY, 2016

The morning sunrise behind the Capitol Building in our nation's capital was one for the books. The image graced most of the news shows I saw as I flipped through them while getting ready for work. The Capitol was lit by white lights in the front and the ruby-gold glow of the sunrise on every other side . . . .

"Embraced it, ensconced it. The image was beautiful and inspiring." Had I been a writer for a paper, those would have been my words, for that was what I saw.

As I clicked through the shows, I saw the same image; only the words varied. What came best to mind were Morning Joe on MSNBC and both the weather guy and the anchor on CNN:

> MORNING JOE: "Brilliant sunrise around the Capitol . . . makes you think of all of the history . . . the generations that have come before us and will come after us . . . reminds us that we are a great Nation that will endure . . . . Beautiful picture."
>
> CNN WEATHER GUY: "Isn't that gloomy? I don't want to go there, but what is the old sailor's warning? Just look at the red sky . . . ."
>
> CNN ANCHOR: " 'Red sky at morn, sailor take warn' I think that is what you are going for. Gloomy indeed."

Same day.

Same morning.

Same site.

Same sunrise.

But they did not see the same thing. Well, they did see the same thing, but they saw it through different filters.

I saw a beautiful image of a sunrise behind a building. Not just any building — one that was built when our nation was really just a toddler. One whose great size did not match the size of the nation at that time. But even then, Americans were prone to "go big."

A foreign army burned this Capitol before work on its center dome even began. Then construction was put on hold as states took up arms against each other a few decades later. Where parades of cannon had once rolled in front of it, in that era cannons were pointed at it from over the river and through the woods. The building sat unfinished — watching as its nation tore itself apart. Since then, this Capitol has seen "riot and unruly" — inside and out. But it has also heard the voices of our great minds and the echo of their words over time. Its dome can still bring awe to the faces of children bored with any trip.

It has seen war and peace.

Depression and recovery.

Good times and bad.

What I saw that day was a building that has under its belt the broad view of 230 years. No American alive today has seen half of what it has seen.

I saw a building that has gone through so much of such weight that it might look at the strife of today and shrug.

While many see a patient bleeding-out, the Capitol sees a scraped-knee.

While many see a one-party government and the excuse to push their own plan, the Capitol reflects on the many dialogues it has hosted and thinks, "not so fast."

Whether you believe today will bring good or ill, the Capitol stands bias-free.

Whether you believe our nation today faces the start of something good, or the end of it all, the Capitol remains open.

Whether you believe your voice will or will not be heard by men, the Capitol hears.

Whether you woke up to a new morning or a new mourning, the Capitol remains ready to greet the next sunrise.

Whatever your hopes or fears are for today, tomorrow, and the next four-to-eight years, the Capitol — and its calm sense of perspective — will not vary.

And that is just one more thing that is right with America.

~ 21 ~

View From a Far Land

Debra Kornfield

Pearl S. Buck's book, *Come, My Beloved,* came out in 1953, a year before I was born in Guatemala in the midst of a CIA-backed coup that for years stopped democratic elections there. In her book, Buck tells of three generations of an American family with ties to India. The father tries to do good from New York. His son makes the choice to live in India but holds fast to the ways of his own land. The grandson weds an Indian and lives in a small town there.

I have thought about Buck's tale and how it is like and not like the way I feel and act toward the U.S. I watched a change within the missionary generations of my family. My mom and dad tried to raise us as North Americans, a hard task since we lived in a small out-of-the-way town in Guatemala that spoke Ixil, a Mayan tongue with no alphabet. Mom and Dad learned Ixil, wrote it down, taught folks to read, and gave them the best book, the Bible, in their own tongue.

For a time, as a teen, I lived in Mexico. In college in the U.S., my best friends were TCKs ("third culture kids") like me. In fact, I wed one of them. Though he was born and grew up in Bolivia, he had more of a pledge to the U.S. than I did. Dave and I lived with our kids in Brazil for 20 years. Our youngest daughter wed a Brazilian. We have been to and have friends in many lands, near and far.

Thus, when I think of patriotism, my view may seem strange to U.S.-bred ears. I first think of Jesus, who said the Good News would be preached in all lands. This means I have brothers and sisters in all of the world. My first pledge is to them and to their Lord and mine, King Jesus. When he comes back to earth, the lines drawn on maps that split us will have no weight. Wars will cease. Love will reign so all will be safe and free and have food and health.

Until then, the thought of my brothers and sisters in the world leaves me with no strong tie to just one land. I have seen both good and bad done by my land to folks far and near. God loves all, not one more than or less than He loves me. (See Romans 2:11; James 2:9, 3:17.) He calls us to love and to be kind and to live in peace. God's goal is not for the church to rule a land, but for the growth of His love in all the world. We are charged to care for the earth and for each other, not to gain power over the world.

One thing the U.S. got right is the plan of split church and state, which leaves us free to live as God asks us to. We would not like it if a faith not our own came to rule our land and force us to do what their laws say. So, we should not make folks live by our ways or our church.

Jesus said, "My Kingdom is not of this world" (John 18:36). So we share the Good News in the way Colossians 4:5-6 and 1 Peter 3:15-16 tell us, not by force or by law but by the way we live and love. We show that we are kind, with lives full of joy and peace and all the fruit of the Spirit. We need not fear the loss of our way of life, for this world is not our home (Hebrews 11:13).

In my view, we will do what is right for all, not just for us and what we like at this time. We will win the world through grace, not force. When our hearts are pure, we won't use wrong acts and speech to bring about what we think are right ends.

Jesus taught that what we say flows from what is in our hearts. (See Matthew 12:35, Luke 6:45.) In His time, he did not work to end Roman rule. He worked to free folks from sin's harm to their souls. He spent time with those who sinned. He loved them. His harsh words were for those who thought they were right with God but did not put God's love first or in fact care for those in need of grace.

Our land has so much good in it. But I fear we may lose it, not from acts by folks who are not like us, but by those of our own faith who want to force our ways on them. This is not God's plan. I love James's words that show us what makes God's heart glad and grows good fruit from seeds of peace. (See James 3:13-18.) I want to use the gifts God gave me to bless in every way I can and see this take place in the church in each place where the church can be found.

To best serve my land, I look for good fruit in those who lead, which means I will not vote for speech that hurts or words that lie. I must not vote for acts that make God seem far from the poor or ban those who need love and Good News. I want to use my zeal to try to heal wounds and to build — not to hurt or tear down — what folks make through their hard work.

Yes, to best bless my own land, I pledge to act and speak with love from my heart for those from any place. Like Jesus did.

~ 22 ~

A True Patriot

Lin Daniels

When I think of patriotism, my mind goes straight to Ryan P. Jones. I knew him as a young boy, whom I taught in my elementary-school gym class. Full of life, he also had a quick smile and was light on his toes.

With the help of an ROTC scholarship, Ryan went to college and was soon a lieutenant in the army. While in Baghdad, his mind often turned to thoughts of his small hometown — Westminster, Massachusetts. With a total of no more than 8,000 people, it was a close-knit bunch. So, Ryan sent a letter to the elementary school, in search of a class to be his "pen pal."

Mrs. Collins' kindergarten class jumped at the chance. They could not wait to hear from him and with eager pens wrote him back. A bond of love had begun.

The kindergarten kids sent Ryan a book called "Remembering the Heroes" while Ryan, for his part, gave each child in the class a patch with a reverse American flag. A flag of that type stands for Assaulting Forward and can be traced back to Civil War days. The idea was to move on and not draw back under fire.

One day, when Ryan was 23, the letters stopped. All were in shock as we heard that Ryan had died from an IED in Iraq.

At Ryan's wake, his parents spoke of his growth and faith. He often led Bible study and prayer with the men under his care, to prep them for their duty. He had a true sense of the risk they would face. Yet he knew God stood by them in the midst of their days.

Because they knew the place it held in their only child's heart, after Ryan died, his parents came to Mrs. Collins class. They brought a few items that he had held dear to share with his pen pals. Ryan's parents took a photo of the class and gave each child a notebook to write about each of their next 12 years in school. They also pledged a $1,000 scholarship to a Massachusetts state school for each child, as they shared what they wrote from K-12. What a way to honor Ryan and keep him alive in the next generation!

Ryan held a deep love for the United States — in being ready to serve in a far-away land and even die there so that his kindergarten pen pals could live in a free world.

In all our eyes, Ryan P. Jones was a true patriot.

~ 23 ~
I Love America

Debbie Jansen

Our American past is filled with patriots. Most lost all they had in order to save freedom. I can't last more than a few days without a prayer of thanks for them. The thought of their lives fills my mind and moves me to tears. I love America, and live my life so as to reflect my country's zeal.

Patriots move me to be my best. Their firm will sweeps away gloom and cries out for my pledge to stand with them and their cause. Freedom is the total of all that is good. I shout what I feel about freedom not by what I wear or say, but in what I do.

When the church bells ring, their peals bring to mind the tales of the fight for freedom to worship God that the first people who came to this land waged. Pilgrims gave their all; some even died for their stand for God. They faced great loss to launch our American way of life.

The Declaration of Independence ends with the words "We pledge to each other our lives, our fortunes, and our sacred honor." All 56 men who signed The Declaration had to flee for their lives because they were called traitors. Most were barred from their families or homes. Nine died of wounds or lack of help during the war. Five were seized, jailed, and beaten. Their families were left with no money, picked on, jailed, or killed. One signer was forced from his wife's side while she was dying. His children had to flee and were never seen again. Seventeen men who signed the Declaration lost all they owned. The homes of 12 of the men were burned to the ground.

Even though bribed with safety, they held fast to their honor, true to their pledge and their country. Why? Liberty is at the heart of a blessed life. Freedom matters. As Patrick Henry told the Virginia Assembly, "Give me Liberty or Give me death!"

When I see the hills and vales of rich farmland, I think of those who strove to grow crops in this country amid green, lush fields and clear streams. They stood firm amid pain, hard work, and threats of death through the power of hope and the dream of a good life.

When Hitler and Stalin killed millions of Jews, American patriots felt stir within them the love of freedom for all. This time, our men cried out, "Give *them* liberty or give us death."

We may put our hands over our hearts when we see the American Flag. We may wave at soldiers as they march in a parade. We may stand for the National Anthem at a game. And that may be where our devotion to country stops. But a patriot will always ask, "What can I *do* or *give* to *preserve* Freedom?"

When I think of so many who have risked their lives for our country, I want to pass on our patriotism to my children and grandchildren. When I look at their sweet faces, I am dead set on saving freedom so they will not live in chains. I teach them about how great America is and I strive to bring good people into our shared lives. I make sure they know that things of worth come with a price and that truth and history are our best hope. I help them do what is right even when it is hard and praise them when they act with honor. I soothe them when they are hurting, and urge them to trust our faith to guide each next step.

As Americans, we have survived hard times and tamed our trials. But, in the end, it is our patriots who keep us safe and free. Today's patriot is a hard worker, a good friend, and a person filled with love and fire for America. That patriot will give their all to protect freedom. The life I see that patriot live is why I can feel patriotic as well. Thank you, good men and women of America. Thank you for all you do to keep freedom.

Freedom doesn't come cheap. To stand up for a free country may call for all that I am or have. Will I give my life for it? Yes!

Yankee Doodle Boy
by George M. Cohan (1904)

I'm a Yankee Doodle Dandy,
A Yankee Doodle do or die;
A real live nephew of my Uncle Sam's.
Born on the Fourth of July.
I've got a Yankee Doodle sweetheart,
She's my Yankee Doodle joy.
Yankee Doodle came to London,
Just to ride the ponies,
I'm a Yankee Doodle boy.

I'm the kid that's all the candy,
I'm a Yankee Doodle Dandy
I'm glad I am!
So's Uncle Sam!

I'm a real live Yankee Doodle,
Made my name and fame and boodle,
Just like Mister Doodle did by riding on a pony

I love to listen to the Dixie Strain,
I long to see the girl I left behind me;
And that ain't a josh, she's a Yankee, by gosh!

Oh, say can you see...
Anything about a Yankee that's a phony?

I'm a Yankee Doodle Dandy!
A Yankee Doodle Do or Die!
A real live nephew of my Uncle Sam's
Born on the Fourth of July!

I've got a Yankee Doodle Sweetheart
She's my Yankee Doodle Joy

Yankee Doodle came to London
Just to ride the ponies,
I am a Yankee Doodle Boy!

I'm a Yankee Doodle Dandy!
A Yankee Doodle Do or Die!

A real live nephew of my Uncle Sam's
Born on the Fourth of July!

I've got a Yankee Doodle Sweetheart
She's my Yankee Doodle Joy

Yankee Doodle came to London
Just to ride the ponies,
I am that Yankee Doodle Boy!

~ 24 ~
These Things We Hold Dear

Kenneth Avon White

On July 20, 1969 at 10:39 P.M. Neil Armstrong sprung loose the lunar ship's hatch and stepped onto the alien ground of a new world. Just prior to this giant leap for man, Mama had woken us kids up, plopped us down in front of the TV and in hushed tones told us our minds would never lose sight of what we were about to see. Mama was right.

The thought that NASA's brain — the one that ran the whole feat — was just on the other side of Houston from where we lived made this American dream-come-true all the more out of this world. That night I first felt in my bones what America means to me. It was as if the soul of America spoke to mine to plant this seed of truth: In America dreams come true.

At the time I was a young sprout of nine. Up to this point, my only sense of what America is, what it seeks to be, and what that might mean to me were what I had learned in school. My only act of patriotism was when I took part in the Pledge of Allegiance first thing every school day.

A few years later, I tore into my teen years with fierce ardor. My focus was on the "now" and how I could squeeze every bit of life out of life. As I grew into a young adult, my aim was to try out any new thing I came upon. I was free to probe the lures of youth since I lived in America and not some strange land where I would be forced to work a field, labor in a sweat shop, or fight a war I didn't sign up for. Selah.

When the clouds of those naïve years cleared and what was left of my mind's wit began to shine through, I went back to school. I sought to wrap up my Bachelor of Arts at The American University in Washington, D.C. I did not expect to be schooled in America's grand story at the same time.

My major was Radio, TV, and Film. I was taught to go forth ... "film and write about what you see." To tell tales of what drew my eye and how it made me feel. And so, I did for about three years. I did not have a car so I walked the streets filled to the brim with sagas from our past and our growth into a super power. I would sift through the maze of monuments that froze time so we could ever keep in mind what had taken place. I toured the homes of patriots past. I sang songs of glory on the National Mall each 4th of July as the National Symphony played and sparks of color blazed in the sky.

I caught it all through my eager lens.

I'm so glad I didn't have a car those first years in our nation's Capital. For I find when I whiz by a thing or a being it's easy to get caught up in all the noise that can tug and pull on ones' life, and thus miss the hope to be found in each story. In America's story, I found much hope that will float to the top if given a chance. Selah.

Later in life, as I crossed state lines by car going where my work took me, I learned that this opus we call Washington, D.C. had its rival. In the wings along the back roads of this blessed land I found many a great story that fed into this epic we call the U.S.A. I saw up close the great American ideal stretched from farm to farm, small town to small town: Graves of the dead who fought in wars, marched for rights, and those who dreamed big and won. Old Glory painted on the sides of barns. "Don't Tread on Me" flags flown from the back of trucks. Actors who, dressed in clothes of the day, took folks on trips through the local area's past. A cross or two or three perched on the side of a hill. Arts and crafts under rows of tents that oozed with yarns my lens never had the thrill to see. Signs that urged one to vote, which made me think, *Thank you, God, that I have the right to choose and vote.* Selah.

America is a place where every one of us is free to be. Here we can praise the great "I Am" with no fear of a doomed fate. In this place, hope still blooms if folks — even with ideas that vary — can still lock arms and take a look at where the road could lead. In America, the best of all things is baked into the soil. But at times we have to dig to find that good in the place where it lies like water trapped down below, ready to morph into a well that springs forth with the fluid of life. Here the worst of all things can be licked should we, as one, hold tight to these truths that most of us hold dear. Selah.

~ 25 ~
I Am Free

Michelle Newman

I am free.

I can think.
I can speak.
I can disagree.

I don't need to fear
That they will hear
What I say,
And twist it to be
Against the state.

No need to fear
A snitch — who
To save his own skin,
Or for his mother,
His brother,
His wife or kids,
Would turn in
His neighbor,
His friend.

Is it a choice?
Or a sad must?
Is there ever a choice?

The fear that
With open ears and a smile of lies
He will hear me speak,
Make note of it all,
Pass the news up,
Til I take the fall.

The fear that
One day
I will get a note.

A note that says
I must show up.
And no one,
No one,
Tells them no.

There is no choice.
So, with dread, I go.

In a room of dull gray
They try to lull me,
As if I'm safe.
Like dressed-up snakes,
They try to trap me.

I am charged
With what I said.
I am told
I must bend,
Must deny
What I thought —
My own thoughts
In my own head!

For the good of the whole
But what is good?
We all
Must be the same,
Must be
What we are told to be.

So, do not think.
For sure don't speak.
Tear who you are
Out.
Shut your thoughts
Down.
The state knows best.

Like prey that is stalked,
My heart beats in step
With fear, fear, fear!
If I am weak,
If thoughts blurt out,
They thrust those whom I love
Into harm's way.
So, I dare not
Let my mind roam.

But my soul —
Oh, how have you lived through this?
It still knows truth
Even when it should not.
For in the depth of a soul —
I cannot out loud claim as my own
Lest it be known —
Breathes my wish
Even yet
To be free.

Thu-thump.
Lift.
Soar.

But, I am here
On the other side of things.
My wish then is no mere wish now.
I breathe.
In.
Out.

Pinch me.
Is this real?

I am free.

I can think.
I can speak.
I can even disagree!

And that is what America means to me.

Inspired by *The Berlin Letters* by Katherine Reay, a novel about the Iron Curtain.

~ 26 ~
Home of the Free and the Brave

Liz Kimmel

From the day of my birth until now I have worn many hats and taken on many roles: daughter, grandchild, sister, cousin, friend. When I grew up I added some more: wife, mom, aunt, grandmom. At school, I've been on both sides — the one who learned with her friends and the one who stood in front of the main desk and taught. I've also worked in a store, a café, and a bank. I've used my brush to paint homes. I've been a clerk who kept track of other folks' health charts and later did the same for their money. I served my church for 20 years in too many ways to count.

All these things I have done and been under the flag of the red, white, and blue; the stars and stripes of the U.S.A. I was lucky to be born here and give thanks to God that this is where He chose to plant me.

And every time I moved, that new place was still part of the U.S.A. In fact, my whole life has been lived in the state of Minnesota in its capital city of St. Paul. There, I have met lots of folks from other lands. In fact, many of my friends are from far away: Togo, Congo, Liberia, Haiti, Brazil, Ireland, Scotland, India, and more. In the place of their birth, each of them has risen above things that I have never had to face because I live in the "land of the free and the home of the brave."

Home is where I feel safe, loved, known. Yet truly, one other place is more "home" to me than this land, this city. It's my home to come and for all time — even when my days on earth are done. A hymn I have loved to sing ever since I was a young girl says it best: "This world is not my home, I'm just a-pass'n through. My treasures are laid up somewhere beyond the blue. The angels beckon me from heaven's open door, and I can't feel at home in this world anymore."* But until then, I love my home on earth. I love where it is and those I share it with.

Freedom is what makes the U.S.A. a great place to be. True, some things are going on today that make it seem that we are not as free as we used to be. But I choose to live through the strength of the Spirit of God. And He says, *"If the Son sets you free, you are truly free"* (John 8:36 NLT)." So while I give thanks for being able to walk free as part of the U.S. crowd, I am even more aware of being free in my heart. No chains can bind me, for Jesus and I are linked; our bond can't be split. I am free, yet fully bound to Him.

Scores of brave men and women have gone through trials, toil, and strife to make our country the great land it is today. Strong hearts and hands have worked hard to give the U.S.A. a great Constitution and set of laws. What would my life look like if it weren't for the grit, spunk, and valor of those who have gone ahead of me and paved the way? I know God wants these traits to be a part of my life as well. The Bible verse that has seen me through every high and low is this: *"Be strong and brave! Don't be afraid and don't panic, for I, the* LORD *your God, am with you in all you do"* (Joshua 1:9 NET).

Being patriotic means that I am loyal to all who are in my life — in every city, state, or town where I have lived. I want my whole body to be full of zeal as I seek to make my world civil, kind, and full of grace. I want my whole mind to focus on the faith that has been birthed in me and grows in depth and breadth with each new day. I want my whole heart to be given over to the truth of who I am in Christ, one who lives to serve and love. Every day, I seek to point all I meet toward the God who is my home, sets me free, and makes me brave.

Then, and only then, can I help my country to be that same kind of place for all who live here. May this goal be shared by all who will make their way to these shores.

* "This World Is Not My Home" lyrics by Albert E. Brumley

~ 27 ~
My Uncle George

Michael Shoemaker

When I look at the American flag
I think of Uncle George
who served in the U.S. Navy
during the Cuban Missile Crisis,
did fleet training at Guantanamo Bay.
Quiet, meek, almost always
with a gentle smile.
Uncle George — an American hero.

When I look at its field of blue
I think of right done.
Uncle George gave twenty years
to the Atlanta Police Department;
went through riots, bomb scares,
drug busts, and shoot-outs.
One day with his son and nephew,
at a pool to swim,
he had to share the story about two long scars
on his torso from a knife fight.
Blue-eyed, mustached,
he — an American defender.

When I see its stars
I think of his pure heart,
how I had to listen close to even
hear Uncle George's voice
when he said grace over the food
because it seemed that to him
the only one who needed
to hear his thanks was His Father.
He — an American believer.

Tears drop as I look at the stripes
and think of the valor of spirit and how
Uncle George battled with colon cancer
for two years, never winning always losing
against the tidal wave of pain and ruin
until he could rest his head for the last time
with his wife and daughter looking on,
he — my American fighter.

Anchors Aweigh

Original lyrics by Midshipman First Class Alfred Hart Miles (1906)

Revised Lyrics
by George D. Lottman (1926)

Stand, Navy, out to sea, Fight our battle cry;
We'll never change our course,
So vicious foe steer shy-y-y-y.
Roll out the TNT, Anchors Aweigh. Sail on to victory
And sink their bones to Davy Jones, hooray!
Anchors Aweigh, my boys, Anchors Aweigh.
Farewell to college joys, we sail at break of day-ay-ay-ay.
Through our last night on shore, drink to the foam,
Until we meet once more. Here's wishing you a happy voyage home.

[The following written by Midshipman Royal Lovell, Class of 1926:]

Blue of the Seven Seas; Gold of God's great sun
Let these our colors be Till all of time be done-n-n-ne,
By Severn shore we learn Navy's stern call:
Faith, courage, service true With honor over, honor over all.

~ 28 ~
Just a Patriot

Jim Layton

Some say I am a hero, but I don't think so.

In 1968, North Korea hit the USS Pueblo. They took the ship and the U.S. Navy crew who were aboard. I was one of 83 who were tied, bound so we could not see, and sent to prison. I spent 11 months as a POW in a North Korean war camp.

The crew bore harsh abuse. I was forced to crawl on my knees until they bled and then was kicked to make me walk more. I held a chair over my head until I could not bear it, and they would hit me when it fell. We were fed sour rice, and what we drank was foul. We didn't bathe for months and dwelt in our filth.

Why was there so much hate? I do not know.

In that cell, I felt fury. Why didn't the U.S. save me? I stayed in angst while peace talks lagged on. I could have died there, and America didn't seem to care.

Or was that just what the North Koreans told me?

Sixty years have come and gone. I still ache when thoughts flash through my mind; the smell of rice makes me sick, and I bear deep scars. At times, I close up in my room and shut out the world. God and I talk. He's the one who saw me through it. I didn't know Him then but I know Him now and I am sure He was there.

I could hate the U.S. for the long, drawn-out stay, but I don't. I love America. I didn't choose to be a POW, but I did choose to serve my country. After I came back, I stayed in the Navy for 22 years. I stuck with it and gave a large part of my life and time to service.

Am I a hero? You could say that, but to me, I am just a patriot — one who knows the need for duty to God and country.

~ 29 ~
My United States

Allyson West Lewis

In school, we said the Pledge of Allegiance every day. I loved it. Along with the Lord's Prayer, it was what I could say aloud as a child with no need to peek.

On July 4, 1976, we celebrated the United States' Bicentennial, 200 years of being a self-ruled land. I watched as many kinds of boats sailed or cruised near the Statue of Liberty, all with United States flags set to soar. It gave me chills to be in this great land! My heart leapt!

Time passed. My husband and I took our young son, Stephen, to New York and sailed to the Statue of Liberty in 20° temps that bit right through us. Once on Liberty Island, we saw plaques of the past set out on the grounds and in the Statue of Liberty. She had been a gift from France to make note of the unity between us during the American Revolution. France viewed America as an ally in the fight for liberty and the goals of free speech, free rights, and so much more.

September 11, 2001 began as a day with clear blue skies and mild temps. Too soon, dread grew in me while I talked on the phone to a good friend and colleague. Fear snaked through us as we watched the Wall Street news. We both worked for large firms on Wall Street. When the first tower of the World Trade Center fell, I left work to pick up my fourth-grade son from school and take him home. He went straight to his room to play, which was good. I didn't want him to see the news. Then, along with my father and mother, I watched our world change.

A large number of my colleagues in New York died in those towers. One of them called his wife, who worked in the South Tower, to tell her how much he loved her. Their phone line broke off as that tower went down. Weeks later, a friend and colleague in New York told me how drained he felt from all the last rites he had borne. A time of grief spread over the whole United States.

To this day, as I mourn those who lost their lives, I laud all the brave men and women who rushed *into* each tower to help those trapped inside. From my heart, I thank those other brave men and women who went to fight for our country then and have gone in the years since.

Twenty-four years after I'd left my career on Wall Street, my husband and I went to the 9/11 Memorial and Museum. To this day, I feel chilled to think that six months before the 9/11 attack, I had been in an 8:30 AM work meeting at Windows on the World, located on the top floors (106th and 107th) of the North Tower. The first plane hit the North Tower at 8:46 AM that grim day in 2001. The North Tower collapsed at 10:28 AM.

My thoughts of 9/11 will never fade. Our brave men and women who sign up to stand guard for our America, then and now, fill me with joy.

I am proud to live in this land, this America, these United States.

~ 30 ~
# Much Left to Love

Susan Cheeves King

When I heard the tragic news on September 11, 2001, my first thought was, *We will see heroes.* And we did — on land as men and women stormed into the bowel of hell for the sake of others and in the air when heroes rushed the terrorists so they could not reach their target in Washington D.C. How was I so sure of the deeds to come? Ours is a nation of heroes.

Ever since I was a small child, I have loved the United States of America. And it wasn't just a knee-jerk pride in the place where I live — a kind of "my country, right or wrong." No. While not blind to America's past sins, I could never love a country that is more wrong than right.

The nation I love has to earn my faith, hope, trust, and, yes, fierce love — by being deep and strong, a country that people who don't even live here could love.

Many years ago, this fact about America first showed up on my radar when I had bought an item on eBay and it turned out the seller was in England. How could I pay her? She told me to send the check to her daughter in Temecula, California. When I wrote back how hard it must be for her to live so far from her child, she replied that her son also lived in America, on the east coast. She added, "I do miss them, but it helps for me to know that they are in a far better place." From her words, you would have thought they'd both died and gone to be with God! And it wasn't as if hers was a third-world country. It was just that the U.S. was *that* kind of place — one that people could love above their own homeland.

How could they — how did I — look past our flaws to love America?

As I said to my son, David, after he'd been taught by his history teacher about all of America's past sins, "Our country is like the Lord's church. Because it's made up of people, it can never be perfect, but because it was established under a perfect set of laws, it is certainly better than any other country."

In the case of the church, that *"perfect law of liberty"* (James 1:25 KJV) comes from God, but in the case of America, it came from brave and clear-eyed men who sweat blood to come up with a perfect Constitution and then put all they had on the line — their very lives — for the new country that was pledged to use that law as its guide. These founders that I am so proud of made us a "city set on a hill" by God Himself — that would draw people from all over the world to its shores. It kept America a place that I could honor with my love and trust.

That's when I thought our constitution was safe from the corrupt culture and society that over the past five decades have turned away from God — in ways that I view with shock and disgust. Patriots have watched sacred tenets of belief fall one by one and even the idea of morality or ethics fade away. We live in a time when each person has his own "truth" and even the facts of science can move and change at the whims of the one who yells the loudest or who has the ear of the media.

But even so, I thought I could always look to our seat of government as at least it would hold up the sword of truth and the rule of law.

Not so these days. Now that this base godlessness has marched its loud and proud way into our government, those of us who have always thought of ourselves as patriots have been brought up short. We've had to stand by as the rule of law — a lynch pin of our country (part of what had made our country so great) — is trashed. Some, like me, are asking ourselves, "How many times can my patriot's heart break before it beats its last?"

These days, I haven't felt much like a patriot since I don't see America as the same place that so many brave men and women have fought and died for. My heart and mind have been in a state of crisis that prompts me to take a long look at what I mean by patriotism.

At its core is loyalty and trust. But what is left to be loyal to or to trust when America has morphed into something I don't know anymore? At the least, it has stopped being "the leader of the free world" and "the world's moral compass."

Then the thought struck me that my stress over what is being done to our Constitution and our history and our image in the world had been blinding me to a *tried-and-true* foundation of my patriotism. I take patriotic pride in the character of Americans, the people who every day leave their stamp on the present and the future.

When we talk about the character of a given nation, we do not claim that every citizen of that nation is the exact copy of each other. Our aim is to paint an image of how the citizens of that country *tend* to be, their national identity.

Just as with every other country, sometimes our national traits are best seen by those from without, who can view us with no bias and also match us up next to an image of the people of their lands.

Alexis de Tocqueville, Minister for Europe and Foreign Affairs of France in 1849, was one such person. In his classic work, *Democracy in America*, he sought to nail down an image of the American character. And though he penned his words over 160 years ago, they still hold true today.

Anyone who travels much will catch a less-formal glimpse of how the rest of the world views us. When I taught at a few writers' conferences in Canada — the only American on the faculty — I often heard the Canadians around me state with pride that Canadians are "friendly." When at last I asked about us Americans, they added, "and Americans are fun."

Every semester, on the first day of my American Lit classes, when I asked my college students to brainstorm on the marks of the American character, at least one would call out "entrepreneurial." When, full of thanks, I would ask them to join me as we broke down that multi-syllabled term into words easy to grasp, we would see that the same spirit of our ancestors to sell everything and board boats or wagons to bring them to a home in America fuels us today.

We take risks.

We can see it on a small scale when — only in America — children build and sell out of lemonade stands. We also see it on a large scale in grown-up children like Elon Musk and Bill Gates.

Just as our forebears, we put it all on the line (which is part of why our friends in the rest of the world can depend on us to come through for them). We see life as it is and take risks to make it better.

One key facet of entrepreneurship that Tocqueville saw in us: We don't fear change.

> [In] America... everything is in constant motion and every change seems an improvement. No natural boundary seems to be set to the efforts of man; and in his eyes what is not yet done is only what he has not attempted to do (Tocqueville, *Democracy in America*).

We are also creative, and along with that so sure that if we can think it, we can do it. And Americans find these traits aided by our happy union with an economic system that unleashes the power of the human brain. As American author and radio host Michael Medved phrased it, "Democracy [is] the products of the human mind turned loose by the free market." He went on to point out that the wealth of a country is not in land or material/natural resources, but in ideas.

Tocqueville noted: "Of all the countries in the world, [in] America... the spread of ideas and of human industry is the most continual and most rapid." But what amazed him most was "not so much the marvelous grandeur of some undertakings, as the innumerable multitude of small ones" (*Democracy in America*).

These small "undertakings" occur because Americans have get-up-and-go. We don't let the grass grow under our feet. In this, we are spurred on by another trait of the American character: the Protestant work ethic, the value of hard work for its own sake.

This abundance of energy and will to take action when we see what needs to be done can cause us to "rush in where angels fear to tread" (sorry Alexander Pope) because at times we also have a bit too much heart. As Tocqueville wrote of us, ". . . they are extremely open to compassion" and he went on to note the "great and real sacrifices" Americans make "to lend faithful support to one another: "

> When an American asks for the cooperation of his fellow citizens, it is seldom refused; and I have often seen it afforded spontaneously and with great good will. If an accident happens on the highway, everybody hastens to help the sufferer; if some great and sudden calamity befalls a family, the purses of a thousand strangers are at once willingly opened, and small but numerous donations pour in to relieve their distress. It often happens amongst the most civilized nations of the globe, that a poor wretch is as friendless in the midst of a crowd as the savage in his wilds: this is hardly ever the case in the United States (Tocqueville, *Democracy in America*).

As with many other parts of the American character, the value of hard work and firm pledge to help others spring from our earliest identity as a nation under God. Over and above all else, it is who we have always been as Americans.

From the first, patriots like Ben Franklin wrote about this vital trait of our American character: Christians "preserve and maintain Truth, Common Sense, universal Charity, and brotherly Love, Peace and Tranquility, as recommended in the Gospel of Jesus, in this our infant and growing Nation" (*The Papers of Benjamin Franklin*).

Non-American Tocqueville noted the chasm between France and America, that in France "the spirit of religion and the spirit of freedom [march] in opposite directions" but that in America the two are "intimately united." He went on to point out:

Not until I . . . heard [America's] pulpits flame with righteousness did I understand the secret of her genius and power. America is great because America is good (Tocqueville, *Democracy in America*).

I could go on and on with what I like about who we are as Americans — that we are fresh-faced, earnest, unself-conscious, genuine, and naïve (in the good sense of being trusting and not jaded). And no place in the history of any other nation do we see an image like the tough, bold, and true American Cowboy.

And now that I have been able to shift my focus to pride in the American character, I can reach toward patriotism and once again claim it for myself. For I have seen that the America I love is still here — deep in the hearts of most Americans, the ones who are full of hope and trust and "cock-eyed optimism." My love for them has never stopped, and now I am sure that we can join hands to bring back to life the U.S.A. of old — and once again mean it when we say that we are proud to be Americans.

In the meantime, I do what I should have been doing all along; I place my faith and trust in God first. And, like the persistent widow of Luke 18:1-8, I "pray without ceasing" (1 Thessalonians 5:17 KJV) to a God who already knows our great need and wants our best. God cares for this country that He brought into being, and He has more grace to shed on us.

Humble yourselves . . . under God's mighty hand, that he may lift you up in due time. Cast all your anxiety on him because he cares for you.

1 Peter 5:6-7 NIV

You're a Grand Old Flag
by George M. Cohan

There's a feeling comes a-stealing
And it sets my brain a-reeling
When I'm list'ning to the music of a military band
Any tune like "Yankee Doodle"
Simply sets me off my noodle
It's that patriotic something
That no one can understand
"Way down South in the land of cotton"
Melody untiring
Ain't that inspiring!
Hurrah! Hurrah! We'll join the jubilee
And that's going some
For the Yankees, by gum!
Red, white and blue
I am for you
Honest, you're a grand old flag

You're a grand old flag
You're a high-flying flag
And forever in peace may you wave
You're the emblem of
The land I love
The home of the free and the brave
Ev'ry heart beats true
Under red, white and blue
Where there's never a boast or brag
But should old acquaintance be forgot
Keep your eye on the grand old flag

I'm a cranky hanky panky
I'm a dead square honest Yankee
And I'm mighty proud of that old flag
That flies for Uncle Sam
Though I don't believe in raving
Ev'ry time I see it waving
There's a chill runs up my back
That makes me glad I'm what I am
Here's a land with a million soldiers
That's if we should need 'em
We'll fight for freedom!
Hurrah! Hurrah! For ev'ry Yankee tar
And old G.A.R.
Ev'ry stripe, ev'ry star
Red, white and blue
Hats off to you
Honest, you're a grand old flag

You're a grand old flag
You're a high-flying flag
And forever in peace may you wave
You're the emblem of
The land I love
The home of the free and the brave
Ev'ry heart beats true
Under red, white and blue
Where there's never a boast or brag
But should old acquaintance be forgot
Keep your eye on the grand old flag

~ 31 ~
The Real National Treasure

John Leatherman

I quite like the 2004 movie *National Treasure*. Though the plot falls apart with a slight poke, this smart, wild, action flick is two hours of history-nerd fun.

It brings up a deep point, though. Over two centuries later, why is the original Declaration of Independence so prized that we keep it safe with bulletproof glass, state-of-the-art alarms, armed guards, and CCTV? Even when it was new, it had no great value in and of itself. As Nicolas Cage's Benjamin Gates points out in the film, for the men who signed it, the Declaration of Independence was a death knell.

We laud July 4, 1776, as the birth of the United States of America, but that was just the day some men in a closed room signed a piece of paper in which they dared to defy the king of one of the most powerful countries in the world. Wouldn't it make more sense to have a holiday for Washington's victory over Cornwallis at Yorktown on October 19, 1781? Or what about February 27, 1782 when the British House of Commons voted to stop the fight and grant American independence? Doesn't that seem worth a firework or two? Or if we're going to extol a piece of paper, why wouldn't it be the Treaty of Paris, which laid out the borders of the new nation of the United States of America on September 3, 1783?

Maybe it's just that "Fourth of July" is so much easier to say than "Third of September," "Twenty-seventh of February," or "Nineteenth of October." And 07-04-1776 is a great date if you love seven, as many do. The two non-sevens in the year, one and the six, add up to seven. And what about the four? If you add up the year, you get 21, which adds up to three; add the four and you get seven again!

But maybe there's more to the Fourth than short words and math tricks. American independence could not exist unless our people had the will to put their lives on the line to bring it about. If they were going to fight, they had to see on paper what the fight was for, and then they could "mutually pledge to each other our Lives, our Fortunes and our sacred Honor." So, in a very real way, before any treaty, vote, or war could bring it to life, July Fourth was, in fact, the birth of America.

The back of the real Declaration of Independence doesn't have a treasure map (that I know of). No, the real treasure is right there on the front, where we don't have to search for it — an idea. A principal tenet of freedom that's still worth dying for.

~ 32 ~
This Is America to Me

Heather Holbrook

To praise and pray as I see fit,
Just like my great-grandparents times eleven,
Who came to Plymouth to start again,
That's what America means to me.

To learn a new way of hope in Christ,
Like my Ottawa kin four centuries ago,
Who taught Nicolet how a canoe to row,
That's what America means to me.

To stand up to kings,
Like my great-grandfather times six,
Who died on a British prison ship,
That's what America means to me.

To ban chains from all persons,
Like my ancestor, POTUS two,
Who wrote the Massachusetts State Constitution,
That's what America means to me.

To speak the truth 'til good is done,
Like my line, who urged the south,
Who undid the gag rule meant to quiet his mouth,
That's what America means to me.

To make sure all are free,
Like my blood born at Sinking Spring Farm,
Who was shot for his rule meant to keep black Americans from harm,
That's what America means to me.

To lift up the poor,
Like my stock, FDR,
Who gave work and pride not just hand outs,
That's what America means to me.

To seek life and peace,
Like my great-grandfather from Cosenza,
Who snuck on a boat bound for Ellis Island,
That's what America means to me.

To marry whom you love,
Like my great-grandma, First Nations and French,
Who'd just moved to the Badger State, down from Quebec,
That's what America means to me.

To earn a fair wage for work well done,
Like my great grandpa from the Land of the Midnight Sun,
Who built Minneapolis 'til the sky was won,
That's what America means to me.

To be free to be me,
Like my grandmother, both fair and smart,
Who had an ail that, in groups, kept her in the dark,
That's what America means to me.

To greet those new to this land who,
Like my sires and dames both young and old,
Also have dreams full of hope and bold,
That's what America means to me.

~ 33 ~
One Proud Marine

Glenda Ferguson

Dad was a Marine vet from World War II. He took those proud Marine ways into our home life. Going to town? His shoes had to shine. Out for a Sunday drive? The old car was spic and span. Work at the shop? His pants held a sharp crease.

On Memorial Day, Dad would drive me to town to visit the VFW and buy a fake red poppy with a green wire. He would hook the wire over the arm of the gear shift. That small bloom hung there until the next year when Dad would buy a "fresh" one.

As a young girl, I would gaze at Dad in his Marine photo — at his gear, the crest on his hat, and his huge smile — and think of what an honor it was to have him as my dad.

For most of my life, my dad was my hero, but that was not the case when I was a teen. Then, I thought his life was such a bore. He was 16 years older than my mom, with a huge gap from my age to his. Every time the 60s TV show *Gomer Pyle USMC* came on, Dad would say, "I've walked through those gates on that Marine camp many times." He spoke of basic drills and his jobs on base. To tell you the truth, I did not share his zeal for war times. After I'd heard them over and over, I let his words go in one ear and out the other. What's more, I lost sight of the sense of honor about my dad and even toward his flag.

I had left home to study to be a teacher and was about to take my last exams when I had a call from Mom. "I have bad news," she said. "Your dad suffered a massive stroke."

I didn't make it back home in time.

Dad was laid to rest in his family's plot — with family going back to his great-great grandfather who served in the Civil War. Men from the local VFW fired three rifle shots into the air and blew taps. Then they gave Dad's flag with thirteen folds to my mom.

"Your dad loved you so much," Mom said to me as we stood at his grave, "and he was so proud of you going to college."

Next to Dad's plot lay two stones — for his father and grandfather. "They died just a month apart," Mom told me.

I had never made sense of so much of Dad's story. That day began my search to learn more about his past and what led him to join the Marines.

My dad was six years old when his dad passed away from pneumonia. They think he got sick from his January trek across the state to bury his own father. His death left the family all alone — Dad, his three brothers, a sister, and his mom who was seven months along with the sixth child. Two months later, Dad's mom had a boy who died at the age of three.

Those must have been such sad years.

"Since they didn't have their father to provide for them, they moved again and again," Mom told me.

We were able to track their moves to 19 houses and rooms. In spite of that, we found Dad's first grade photo and school-grades card signed by his father.

In 1939, Dad and each of his five friends dreamed of being a Marine. They went more than 100 miles to take the Marine test. Dad was the only one to pass. Maybe that's why he had a huge smile in his Marine photo. At first, Dad went to Camp Pendleton, California, just like the first part of the Gomer Pyle show. His Marine life began on base as a clerk and then an MP. After Pearl Harbor, he went by ship to the front. At the same time, Dad's three brothers and his brother-in-law were in the Navy and the Army. At the end of the war, he met my mom and after she got out of school, they wed.

As a teacher, I guide my class in the pledge to the flag each day, and on Memorial Day I speak of the poppies and what my dad did during WWII. Now, when I look at Dad as a Marine, I hear the Marines' Hymn and the motto "Semper Fidelis" — Always Faithful. Dad was so proud of his Marine past, and I am so proud of my Marine dad.

In Flanders Fields

Lieutenant Colonel John McCrae, 1872 – 1918
Composed at the battlefront on May 3, 1915
during the second battle of Ypres, Belgium

In Flanders fields the poppies blow
Between the crosses, row on row,
That mark our place, and in the sky
The larks, still bravely singing, fly
Scarce heard amid the guns below.

We are the Dead; short days ago
We lived, felt dawn, saw sunset glow,
Loved and were loved, and now we lie
In Flanders fields.

Take up our quarrel with the foe!
To you from failing hands we throw
The torch; be yours to hold it high!
If ye break faith with us who die
We shall not sleep, though poppies grow
In Flanders fields.

The Marines' Hymn
by Jacques Offenbach / Peter Tomashek

From the Halls of Montezuma
To the shores of Tripoli;
We fight our country's battles
In the air, on land, and sea;
First to fight for right and freedom
And to keep our honor clean;
We are proud to claim the title
Of United States Marine.
Our flag's unfurled to every breeze
From dawn to setting sun;
We have fought in every clime and place
Where we could take a gun;
In the snow of far-off Northern lands
And in sunny tropic scenes,
You will find us always on the job
The United States Marines.
Here's health to you and to our Corps
Which we are proud to serve;
In many a strife we've fought for life
And never lost our nerve.
If the Army and the Navy
Ever look on Heaven's scenes,
They will find the streets are guarded
By United States Marines.

~ 34 ~
The Heart of a Nation

Terry Magness

My Dad was a WWII fighter pilot, shot down three times. In his final mission, he ejected after his plane took a hit, but as the plane spun around into a dive, the tail smacked him in the back and knocked him out before he had fully pulled the parachute chord. The "ace" was in a free fall.

Those who saw the whole thing said that about 100 feet from the ground he seemed to rally some. Though very weak, he tugged the chord and again passed out. Moments later, as the chute began to open his limp body slammed into the ground. As he lay there with acute inner injuries, his back and other bones broken or crushed, his heart stopped. Field medics rushed to the scene. A shot of adrenaline was given to start his heart, but it failed. A frantic try with a second shot worked and his heart began to pump again.

He spent the next three months in a hospital. When his body healed, he was moved to an Army base in Kansas where he trained pilots until the end of his tour of duty. I was born on that Army base the very day the papers were signed and World War II ended — September 2, 1945. Dad's pledge to his country was over, but his soul was never the same.

My Dad was only one among the scores of people who paid a high price to shield this nation and to fight for freedom. Americans, torn from the arms of their loved ones, went on to suffer the bitter effects of a world at war, but they rallied 'round Old Glory — our national symbol of liberty. When at last our men came home, the women who worked to help the war effort left the factory jobs they had filled while the men were away. Americans turned their hearts toward home and family and the honor of country.

In the 1950s, patriotism ran high. In our schools we pledged allegiance to the flag as, with deep and sincere loyalty, we placed our right hands over our hearts. With great pride, we flew our flags over our cities and towns. Students were taught American History and Citizenship. Each school day began with class prayer.

We deemed that God's grace upon us was a large part of what makes this country great.

Then came the 60s and a change began to emerge in thought and stance. Still our nation's leaders believed in the fight against tyranny when freedom was at stake, so we went to the aid of South Vietnam.

My husband was among the 8.7 million Americans who served in the Vietnam era and among the 2.7 million who served in the Republic of Vietnam. He received a Compassionate Deferment to deploy after the birth of our first child. Don left for Vietnam just a few days after Christmas 1967. Our son was seven weeks old, and his dad would be gone a year. As it turned out, Don arrived in Vietnam less than five weeks before the awful Tet Offensive of January 30, 1968. It was a blitz — attacks on areas across South Vietnam all at the same time. Even so, Don and his comrades made it through.

Back in the States, a slice of society made a clear shift toward "self" — a type of freedom at the cost of others. A rising sense grew against this war. Some forgot the religious persecution of England and even the tyranny of Hitler's Germany. They forgot that freedom has a price — that men in this country had fought and died to be set free from English oppression. They forgot that this great nation was founded upon what our Constitution makes clear and our pledge states, that we are "one nation under God, indivisible, with liberty and justice for all." When our troops came home from Vietnam, some were spit upon. Some heard obscenities hurled at them and had things thrown at them. Those who did this missed the truth that the God, who has given us the freedom we enjoy, smiles on a nation whose heart beats with His, who cares and is willing to defend the weak and fight for liberty for the sake of others.

Could it be that our nation is in peril now? With the risky slide away from the love and honor of God we have borne grave loss. The pure love and pledge to one another and to this nation we once held dear is fast fading from view. What if we were to turn again to the God we loved and humbly ask His pardon? What if we were to bow our knees once again to our Creator in meek surrender as did those who founded this nation? Could it be that He would again restore our hearts? Could it be that He would again stretch out His hand and bless this nation?

May it be so. And may God bless America again!

~ 35 ~
Land of the Free, Paid for by the Brave

Jan White

I give thanks to God that I live in the "home of the free, paid for by the brave." When I was in first grade, I learned one of the ways to give thanks to be an American. Every class day began as we students stood by our desks, right hands over our hearts, and faced the flag. Then, with one voice we'd say, "I pledge allegiance to the flag of the United States of American and to the Republic for which it stands, one nation, under God, indivisible with liberty and justice for all." As I grew up and began to study how our country began over 200 years ago, these 31 words were not just words to say — but a vow that spoke to my heart.

With each grade in school, I found out more about the high price men and women have paid in wars to keep America the "land of the free." My thanks for those who laid their lives on the line grew with my age. Now that I am more vocal, I speak up!

As an adult, I always say, "Thank you for serving our country" to soldiers when I see them in their camo or to veterans who wear the cap of their branch of the armed services or a cap that tells the war in which they fought.

When I say the Pledge of Allegiance at football games, civic clubs, or on July 4th or other patriotic holidays, I feel my heart beat soft thumps on the palm of my right hand. Each time — again and again — the thought will rush back to my mind, as fresh as the first time, that I live in the "land of the free, paid for by the brave."

~ 36 ~
My Pledge

Karen Masteller

A few years post 9/11, I sat at my desk and gazed through the window. As I am wont to do each day, I had read the Word and prayed, and my thoughts brewed. Why was I born here? Was there someone like me far away in the Middle East with the same thought: *Why was I born here?* In each case, we may have vowed to love where we live, but I was sad for her. While a hard hand ruled in her land, I was blessed; I could choose to make my pledge to a free land.

I learned from my roots that a vow to fight for our land had been a key ideal for our family. My 4th-great-grandfather, Michael Helfrich, served in the Revolutionary War as a private in the Northampton County Militia from 1780 to 1782. Through the years, more of my kin signed up as well. In World War II, both my father and father-in-law joined the troops in the Army and the Navy. My husband served in the Navy in the Vietnam War. My brother-in-law and uncles also joined the cause for peace in the Army, Navy, Marines, and Air Force. They stood as one with America.

How do I show that I have faith in America? Here was one way. For fun, when my husband and I were wed in 1972, the color scheme was red, white, and blue, and the theme was nautical. The girls' gowns were white with red and blue trim. Each girl held a bunch of red, white, and blue mums. A small blue anchor topped my bunch of white mums. Each gent fit the bill in a black tux with a steel blue shirt. The moms dressed in style as well; each wore the hues of the day. We showed love for our land as we pledged our love and trust as one — 'til death do us part.

As such, my life bears fruit that I love America. With heart, I stand and sing "O say can you see . . . ." With pride, I pledge to the Stars and Stripes. As part of my vow, I signed up to vote and go to the polls. I serve my town and state with vim. In good faith, I pay taxes and heed the laws. In awe, I learn how the U.S. Constitution keeps me safe and free. And when I meet those vets who have served, I thank them for their role to keep America safe.

And, too, God's Word tells me to heed those in charge in the land. Romans 13:1–2 states that God put them in place by His will. If I do not see eye to eye with them, I still trust that God's plan is good. My job is to do the right thing so fear will not rule me. My job, as well, is to pray for those who lead. First Timothy 2:1–2 moves me to go to God to plead for kings and those in charge. May they be led by the One Most High who acts in truth and guides well.

Only for a time, I serve these kings of earth. While I love my land here on earth, I long for a far land to come. With keen faith, I must wait to be with God. I walk this sod for now but yearn for my home with no end in the life to come. There in the next world I will meet the One who rules all, King of Kings and Lord of Lords, the one true God. To Him I will pledge my love and life.

~ 37 ~
The Heart of America

Kim Robinson

Feed the hungry, and help those in trouble.
Then your light will shine out from the darkness,
and the darkness around you will be as bright as noon.

— Isaiah 58:10 NLT

I joined my ship crew at the TV screen and watched in horror as American armies marched into Iraq. What were we doing? Did we really think we would find the center of the terror war there? Was Saddam Hussein the true source of all the awful deeds around the world?

I was on the hospital ship *M/V Africa Mercy*, serving in West Africa with hundreds from over 35 nations. Don't get me wrong; I am not a nurse. (I want people to keep their blood under their skin, please.) I taught English and math to long-term-crew kids. But as I stood beside others who also paid to serve in Africa, I was in shock over what the U.S.A. was doing. And my friends from other nations were not happy with us.

Their words gave me pause. I am American. Is my nation my shame? Would I trade my life here in favor of some other place in the world? Never. I love my country. We have a warm heart that gives and gives and gives. That's why we went to Iraq. We didn't want a second Hitler to rise up and take over. Seventeen times we had waited for our allies to make Hussein stop when he broke his word. Were we the police of the world? No, but we cared. We knew from World War II the harm of a cruel ruler that no one stops. And my deep thanks goes to the men and women who went to Iraq and beyond to keep others, not just Americans, safe. No, I would not turn my back on the USA.

What made me think America is so great when my non-American friends did not? What I saw at the time is still true today.

I like how vital it is to us to make sure war-torn countries get help — food, water, health, homes — and also to keep people safe. In fact, that was a big cause for our going into Iraq. Our heart to care. I love it! Many fine groups that help around the world began in America. In fact, the work of our ship, *M/V Africa Mercy*, came out of America. I know of so many others: Samaritan's Purse, World Vision, Compassion, Save the Children, Africa Inland Mission, Operation Smile, many thousands of missionaries, and more.

As I thought about it, I knew the U.S.A. had a deep heart to care for others, to share God's words of hope and health and to build, not to tear down.

Today, I live on land, back in the States. And I do love it. I love our wood homes, our tree-lined streets, our free schools and libraries. I love our civic unity — food banks, senior centers, sport centers, after-school care for kids — and other kind work here. The towns of my friends in Europe, England, Africa, and Australia do not seem to have this heart to lift up others and freely meet their needs.

On the ship, I also thought how I love hiking in city, state, and national parks. Could I ever give that up? When I can't get to those parks, I love going back in my mind to visit such places again. I have heart-warming photos of hiking with my son in the red-rock glory of Zion Park in Utah, of riding the river through the Grand Canyon — as my mom and my kids hung on to the raft and looked up at the wind-carved cliffs above us. Such joy! I have roamed the paths of Yellowstone with my daughter and her kids and have hiked with awe in the Grand Tetons with friends. My nation keeps beauty and nature in vast park lands for all of us to enjoy now and in the future. We love the rich lands God gave us and we share them! And my heart is full of thanks for the many unpaid workers who keep clear the trails I wander. I live in a land of volunteers.

Where else would you go to shop for food and have a chance to buy part of a holiday meal for a family in need? Where else would you find neighbors who bring food to the sick, drive the hurt to the hospital, and care for pets when the owner is away? While God calls His church to act in these ways the world over, in America this is a way of life — Christian or not.

I have lived in more than thirteen countries. And do you know what? I love my U.S.A. best.

America the Beautiful
by Katharine Lee Bates (1893)

O beautiful for spacious skies,
For amber waves of grain,
For purple mountain majesties
Above the fruited plain!
America! America!
God shed his grace on thee
And crown thy good with brotherhood
From sea to shining sea!

O beautiful for pilgrim feet
Whose stern, impassioned stress
A thoroughfare of freedom beat
Across the wilderness!
America! America!
God mend thine every flaw,
Confirm thy soul in self-control,
Thy liberty in law!

O beautiful for heroes proved
In liberating strife,
Who more than self their country loved
And mercy more than life!
America! America!
May God thy gold refine
Till all success be nobleness
And every gain divine!

O beautiful for patriot dream
That sees beyond the years
Thine alabaster cities gleam
Undimmed by human tears!
America! America!
God shed his grace on thee
And crown thy good with brotherhood
From sea to shining sea!

~ 36 ~
What Patriotism Means to Me

Patricia Huey

When I was in the eighth grade, our teacher told us we would write a speech on patriotism with the theme: "What America Means to Me." The speeches would be judged, and the first-place speech would win a medal. The pupil who won would give the speech in front of the Lion's Club. Some of my peers rolled their eyes and groaned. But I loved the chance to enter even though I knew I could never give my speech to the Lion's Club. It scared me to think of my words being sized up by a group of stern-faced older men. Ah, well, I'd worry about that later. . . .

I yearned for that medal, so I set out to win. With songs like *God Bless America, My Country Tis of Thee*, and *America the Beautiful* on my mind, I left for the library, where I would search for other views on the topic. I knew what I felt for the land of my birth, but I was not sure how to put it on paper.

For years, Mrs. Heathcoat, the local librarian, had helped me quench my thirst for books. She seemed pleased to help me find the right ones for my speech topic as well. I couldn't carry all the books home, so she held them until a day when I had a ride.

That first day, I walked out with just a few of the best.

Early on, I learned what American patriotism is not. While some folks wrap up Flag Day, Memorial Day, and Independence Day in red, white, and blue, I found patriotism to be much more than that. Most of us love hot dogs, ice cream, and apple pie; but I began to see that kind of ardor as no more than the love of a fun event and good food. I learned that others put blind faith in our Congress, but that also didn't seem right. No, patriotism was not just being able to vote. So, I searched for more clues.

These days, some might not agree with this thought, but as I read, I learned that America truly is the best nation on earth. Many left their lands of birth to live in America. I read that after most came to America, they ended up with the sense that they could, at last, be free to live without fear. Many longed for a chance to worship as they wished. They had heard that they could reach their goals if they worked hard.

After a second trip to the library, I took more books home. From those I learned that President Washington, in his Farewell Address, said that "religion and moral values" are the "firmest props" to allow a country to stand the test of time. I ran across a French historian, Alexis De Tocqueville, who searched for why America proved most rare of all the nations on earth. His visit to America's churches told him why America is one of a kind. He said, "America is great because America is good, and if America ceases to be good, America will cease to be great" (*Democracy in America*).

As an eighth-grade Christian, I knew I loved my country in part due to the "goodness" I saw in my own church. I loved each man and woman in our church family for their strong faith and moral views. They truly loved America. It was clear to me that the core of America was found in them.

My speech won first place. To my alarm, I was told I must give it in front of the Lion's Club. No speech, no medal. The day of the speech came, and I was a wreck. My mom had made a nice peach-colored dress for me to wear. I thought I looked like an idiot; it was October, and I felt akin to the Great Pumpkin. But what could I say other than, "Thanks, Mom"?

I stood before the group of stern-faced men and shook. I tried to calm down since at this point I was only one step away from my goal to win the medal. At first, my voice also shook as I began my speech: "America is the greatest nation on earth, and these are the reasons." But I had learned that if every day my country gives me the joy of life, I should fight for it — even die for it, if I must. Since right then I felt as though I might die, I steeled myself to be brave. *I will look each person in the eye and give the speech*, I told myself. And I did.

In the end, the club members smiled, stood, and clapped with gusto. At last, when the medal was pinned on me, I felt a thrill like no other.

While that eighth-grade speech is long lost, what I gleaned as I wrote it changed my thoughts. Patriotism is the love of country. If I love America, won't I guard what we all love most about it: "freedom, liberty, and the pursuit of happiness?"

In a small way, our family has done that. My husband was a naval officer. This meant that often I had to rear our son alone while his dad was away for six months at a time, then home for a short while, only to leave again on the next tour of duty. Our son often missed his dad, but he lived among his Navy friends whose dads also loved the U.S. and served it well.

John Adams, the second President of the U.S., said that children should be educated and instructed in the "principles of freedom." I have to agree with him and was glad to learn about those "principles" in my family, my church and my school. I still have the medal I won in eighth grade. But it was not the true prize. The real prize I gained back then was the gift of patriotism that I still hold in my heart today.

Declaration of Independence (Excerpts)

IN CONGRESS, JULY 4, 1776

THE UNANIMOUS DECLARATION OF THE THIRTEEN UNITED STATES OF AMERICA, When in the Course of human events, it becomes necessary for one people to dissolve the political bands which have connected them with another, and to assume among the powers of the earth, the separate and equal station to which the Laws of Nature and of Nature's God entitle them, a decent respect to the opinions of mankind requires that they should declare the causes which impel them to the separation.

We hold these truths to be self-evident, that all men are created equal, that they are endowed by their Creator with certain unalienable Rights, that among these are Life, Liberty and the pursuit of Happiness.–That to secure these rights, Governments are instituted among Men, deriving their just powers from the consent of the governed, –That whenever any Form of Government becomes destructive of these ends, it is the Right of the People to alter or to abolish it, and to institute new Government, laying its foundation on such principles and organizing its powers in such form, as to them shall seem most likely to effect their Safety and Happiness. Prudence, indeed, will dictate that Governments long established should not be changed for light and transient causes; and accordingly all experience hath shewn, that mankind are more disposed to suffer, while evils are sufferable, than to right themselves by abolishing the forms to which they are accustomed. But when a long train of abuses and usurpations, pursuing invariably the same Object evinces a design to reduce them under absolute Despotism, it is their right, it is their duty, to throw off such Government, and to provide new Guards for their future security.–Such has been the patient sufferance of these Colonies; and such is now the necessity which constrains them to alter their former Systems of Government. The history of the present King of Great Britain is a history of repeated injuries and usurpations, all having in direct object the establishment of an absolute Tyranny over these States. . . .

We, therefore, the Representatives of the united States of America, in General Congress, Assembled, appealing to the Supreme Judge of the world for the rectitude of our intentions, do, in the Name, and by Authority of the good People of these Colonies, solemnly publish and declare, That these United Colonies are, and of Right ought to be Free and Independent States; that they are Absolved from all Allegiance to the British Crown, and that all political connection between them and the State of Great Britain, is and ought to be totally dissolved; and that as Free and Independent States, they have full Power to levy War, conclude Peace, contract Alliances, establish Commerce, and to do all other Acts and Things which Independent States may of right do. And for the support of this Declaration, with a firm reliance on the protection of divine Providence, we mutually pledge to each other our Lives, our Fortunes and our sacred Honor.

THE U.S. CONSTITUTION: PREAMBLE

The preamble sets the stage for the Constitution It clearly communicates the intentions of the framers and the purpose of the document. The preamble is an introduction to the highest law of the land; it is not the law. It does not define government powers or individual rights.

Establish Justice is the first of five objectives outlined in the 52-word paragraph that the Framers drafted in six weeks during the hot Philadelphia summer of 1787. They found a way to agree on the following basic principles:

"We the People of the United States, in Order to form a more perfect Union, establish Justice, insure domestic Tranquility, provide for the common defense, promote the general Welfare, and secure the Blessings of Liberty to ourselves and our Posterity, do ordain and establish this Constitution for the United States of America."

(See Archives.gov).

THE U.S. BILL OF RIGHTS

NOTE: The following text is a transcription of the first ten amendments to the Constitution in their original form. These amendments were proposed on September 15, 1789 and ratified December 15, 1791. They form what is known as the "Bill of Rights."

AMENDMENT I

Congress shall make no law respecting an establishment of religion, or prohibiting the free exercise thereof; or abridging the freedom of speech, or of the press; or the right of the people peaceably to assemble, and to petition the Government for a redress of grievances.

AMENDMENT II

A well regulated Militia, being necessary to the security of a free State, the right of the people to keep and bear Arms, shall not be infringed.

AMENDMENT III

No Soldier shall, in time of peace be quartered in any house, without the consent of the Owner, nor in time of war, but in a manner to be prescribed by law.

Amendment IV

The right of the people to be secure in their persons, houses, papers, and effects, against unreasonable searches and seizures, shall not be violated, and no Warrants shall issue, but upon probable cause, supported by Oath or affirmation, and particularly describing the place to be searched, and the persons or things to be seized.

Amendment V

No person shall be held to answer for a capital, or otherwise infamous crime, unless on a presentment or indictment of a Grand Jury, except in cases arising in the land or naval forces, or in the Militia, when in actual service in time of War or public danger; nor shall any person be subject for the same offence to be twice put in jeopardy of life or limb; nor shall be compelled in any criminal case to be a witness against himself, nor be deprived of life, liberty, or property, without due process of law; nor shall private property be taken for public use, without just compensation.

Amendment VI

In all criminal prosecutions, the accused shall enjoy the right to a speedy and public trial, by an impartial jury of the State and district wherein the crime shall have been committed, which district shall have been previously ascertained by law, and to be informed of the nature and cause of the accusation; to be confronted with the witnesses against him; to have compulsory process for obtaining witnesses in his favor, and to have the Assistance of Counsel for his defence.

Amendment VII

In Suits at common law, where the value in controversy shall exceed twenty dollars, the right of trial by jury shall be preserved, and no fact tried by a jury, shall be otherwise re-examined in any Court of the United States, than according to the rules of the common law.

Amendment VIII

Excessive bail shall not be required, nor excessive fines imposed, nor cruel and unusual punishments inflicted.

Amendment IX

The enumeration in the Constitution, of certain rights, shall not be construed to deny or disparage others retained by the people.

Amendment X

The powers not delegated to the United States by the Constitution, nor prohibited by it to the States, are reserved to the States respectively, or to the people.

The Gettysburg Address

Four score and seven years ago our fathers brought forth on this continent, a new nation, conceived in Liberty, and dedicated to the proposition that all men are created equal.

Now we are engaged in a great civil war, testing whether that nation, or any nation so conceived and so dedicated, can long endure. We are met on a great battle-field of that war. We have come to dedicate a portion of that field, as a final resting place for those who here gave their lives that that nation might live. It is altogether fitting and proper that we should do this.

But, in a larger sense, we can not dedicate – we can not consecrate – we can not hallow – this ground. The brave men, living and dead, who struggled here, have consecrated it, far above our poor power to add or detract. The world will little note, nor long remember what we say here, but it can never forget what they did here. It is for us the living, rather, to be dedicated here to the unfinished work which they who fought here have thus far so nobly advanced. It is rather for us to be here dedicated to the great task remaining before us – that from these honored dead we take increased devotion to that cause for which they gave the last full measure of devotion – that we here highly resolve that these dead shall not have died in vain – that this nation, under God, shall have a new birth of freedom – and that government of the people, by the people, for the people, shall not perish from the earth.

Abraham Lincoln
November 19, 1863

About the Authors

Carol Baird's (p. 42) stories and poems are inspired by her memories and her relationship with Jesus Christ.

Her work has been included in several anthologies including a poem in *Cool-inary Moments* (for Divine Moments book series), an online devotion in Christian Devotions.us, and a non-fiction piece in *Mishaps and Misadventures* (for the Short and Sweet series).

She is a member and past treasurer of Word Weavers, Volusia County. Carol organized and hosted a church poetry group. She writes rhymed poetry, devotionals, and Bible studies.

Carol is a wife, mother, grandmother, and great grandmother. Card crafting is her hobby. She has taught study groups and workshops, spoken at Women's Ministry, taken part in a lay evangelism program, and worked on a Co-Labor Core during a Billy Graham Crusade.

With an Army veteran father and a U.S. Navy nurse mother, **Jeff Brady** (pp 20, 77) has always taken a keen interest in American history. Educated as a History teacher, he spent a few years in the classroom and has since worked in industries ranging from videogames to music to textbooks. While those pay the bills, traveling our country and finding the "good" in his fellowman are his true passions.

Jeff considers it a great vacation to venture to an oft-forgotten historical marker that tells a story worth sharing, for, as Jeff says, "The path less taken often has the best stories." He has proven that over and over again in his Facebook posts about "What Is Right With America" and his blog at www.wirwa.com.

Eddie Burchfield (p. 60) was born on August 10, 1950, to Edward C. and Margaret L. Burchfield, both WWII veterans. The family lived in Bessemer, Alabama and included Edward and two younger siblings — a sister and a brother. The three shared a great childhood with lots of love in their house.

After graduating from Bessemer High School, Edward was drafted into the United States Army during Vietnam where he served two years active duty, and seven years in the Army National Guard. He is married and has two children. In 2015, Edward retired from the Alabama Department of Transportation after working there for 32 years. Since his retirement, he has been working in full time in ministry as an Evangelist and Chaplain with the Church of God Chaplains Commission.

Rachel Coggins (p. 18) retired as an Army Reserve Chaplain after serving for 25 years. During her service, she deployed four times for war support in difficult and challenging situations. *Gateway to Iraq, A Chaplain's Story*, is her book about one of these deployments. Rachel's husband was an active-duty Air Force chaplain for 28 years. The military moved them to many locations where they enjoyed a variety of cultures and scenery.

The Coggins reside in the panhandle of Florida. They enjoy the area's beauty and the wonderful people who live there. Rachel finds healing and solace through gardening, writing, and raising butterflies and chickens. She and her husband are active members of their church and often provide counsel to those with military backgrounds.

Pamela Cosel (p. 28) is a co-writer of the Amazon bestsellers, *Return of Christ: The Second Coming* and *Jesus to Jesus*, both focused on promoting peace and interfaith harmony.

Pam is a writer and editor first published as a journalist in 1980. She has written for newspapers, magazines, and for television news in Colorado and Texas. Pam covered the Democratic National Convention in Denver in 2008 for KXRM, the year Barack Obama won the presidential nomination. She has also worked in communications with United Way and Hospice.

Her background includes 14 years of work in city government in communication, special events management, and tourism. She now writes from home, with a focus on her freelance business, ATXEditing.

She lives in Eureka, California near her daughter. Her sons live in Colorado and Texas.

Jennifer Cotney (p. 58) is an award-winning poet and writer, and the cofounder of Christian Mix 106. Though her passion is poetry, she also writes Christian fiction and devotions and contributes to various faith-based blogs and magazines. Jennifer is an active member of Christian Women In Media, Women Fictions Writers of America, and The Southern Christian Writers Guild. She also hosts The Weekend Free For All, a weekly program featuring new releases in Christian music and the highest-rated music program on Christian Mix.

A graduate of Reinhardt University in Waleska, Georgia, Jennifer lives in New Orleans with her family. With a heart for rescue — animal and human — she can be found volunteering at a local animal shelter or serving "the least of these" in her local community.

After 39 years of teaching physical education, mostly at the elementary school level, **Lin Daniels** (p. 83) retired. For the past seven years, she has enjoyed writing, preaching on occasion, and working with the youth group at church. An avid golfer, she plays with her twin sister several days a week. They especially delight in playing as partners and dress almost identically except for one small item (maybe a different color hat)! "After all," she says, "you have to 'zig and zag' a bit as teammates."

Another of Lin's passions is pickle ball — a tennis-like game played on a smaller court with a whiffle ball. Lin gives thanks to God for the depths of His love as well as all the surprises He has graciously bestowed on her.

Bonnie Evans (p. 9) was raised in a Christian home but was 23 before she understood the heartbeat of the gospel: Jesus didn't just die for the world; He died for *her*. Through solid church teaching, Bible studies, fellowship with believers, and regular quiet time with God, she has steadily grown in His grace ever since then.

She pursues her mission to encourage those going through a long season of hardship and trials by speaking, writing (magazine articles, seven books published, blogs, emails, texts), and hosting workshops that she's created.

Bonnie met her husband, Mike, on a blind date in 1971 and married him six months later. God has blessed them with two wonderful children who are an asset to their communities. Mike and Bonnie live in Ione, California.

After graduating from high school, **Glenda Ferguson** (p. 120) went on to complete education degrees from College of the Ozarks and Indiana University. Since retiring from teaching fourth grade and Indiana history, Glenda has contributed to *All God's Creatures, Angels on Earth, Chicken Soup for the Soul, Reader's Digest, Sasee,* and four books in the *Short and Sweet* series. The Indiana Arts Commission has included her poem "The Buffalo Trace Trail: Then and Now" in the INverse Poetry Archive.

Glenda receives virtual encouragement from the Writers Forum of Burton Kimble Farms Education Center. As a volunteer with Indiana Landmarks, she conducts tours of two historical hotels at the French Lick Resort. Glenda and her husband Tim live in southern Indiana, where they display the American flag on their front porch.

From the time she was placed in a seventh-grade creative-writing class, **Joanne Fleck** (p. 26) knew that she really enjoyed writing. However, it wasn't until fairly late in life that she found a path toward pursuing this calling.

Once she was finally able to get started on her first serious writing project, Joanne's work was slowed down while she and her husband cared for her father, who suffered from dementia. Although it seemed like a delay, Joanne could see God's hand in it. During that time, she learned much about writing skills that could improve the quality of her writing in that project and reflect excellence in every writing project to come. "If You Can Keep It" is her third piece to be published in the *Short and Sweet* series.

Jasmine Gatti (p. 70) is a member of Word Weavers Online Groups and posted three blogs in 2023 for them. She is the author of poetry, articles, and devotionals. Publications include those on *Inkspirationsonline.com,* with forthcoming publications in *Christian Devotions* and a *Divine Moments* anthology. Her articles on topics such as Spirituality and Health and Elder Care have appeared in *American Family Physician.* Her current work includes a caregiving book and devotional series and a collection of poetry. View her website at: Writeinstantly.org

Jasmine received her MA in writing from Johns Hopkins University and her MD from Georgetown University School of Medicine. As a hospice clinician and family and geriatric practitioner; she speaks on caregiving to parents, children, dogs, and patients. She lives in Maryland with her husband, terrier, and grown children.

After college, **Pam Groves** (p. 75) moved from Portland, Oregon to teach school in an isolated rural town. She married fellow teacher, Stan, three months after they met. When their family grew to six adopted children, she chose a new role: stay-at-home mom.

Writing has been a part of her life since elementary school. Her work has been published in 12 of the 13 *Short and Sweet* books. She says that writing for this series has been a fun learning experience — building skills in choosing the best word and cutting what does not move the story forward.

At age 62, Stan passed away from microcystic adnexal carcinoma, a rare form of cancer. During their marriage, Pam and Stan took joy in their family and always trusted that God was with them.

Based in Texas, **Leah Hinton** (p. 64) is a poet, short-story author, screenwriter, and playwright. Among her awards are the McClatchy Fiction Prize for her stories *Blue, Dark Fog,* and *Spin-Me, Charlie*; the Dallas Area Writers Poet's Prize for *Barefoot*, and the 2019 Stage Writers Festival Audience-Choice Spotlight Award for her play, *Ripe*.

Her play, *Paper Thin*, was a feature selection by Imprint Theatre in 2020. Her short films *Lost Man, Bantam,* and *Single* are in production as part of the feature-length anthology, *Dad-Father-Papa,* from Carpe Diem Pictures. Her latest screenplay to be made into a movie, *Broken Chords,* was released in 2022. She is a full member of the Dramatists Guild, Associate Director of Stage Writers, President of the Writers Guild of Texas, Event Liaison of the DFW Writers Room, and founder of R.A.W. Arts Poetry Guild.

Heather Holbrook (p. 118) lives in Shoreview, Minnesota with her husband of 23 years, two cats, and a revolving door of two young adult children, and any number of international college students, scholars and their families.

She has always enjoyed writing. But she also enjoys science, so when trying to decide on a college major, she cried out in desperation to God and he answered, "Write." Heather worked as a technical writer for a medical device company, then "retired" to stay home with her children. She scratched the writing itch with blogging and helping others with their ministry letters, job applications, etc. Now she enjoys tutoring children in writing and has begun to try her hand at poetry and memoir writing. Her hope is that others will be drawn to God through the words He gives her.

Patricia Huey (p. 137) was born in the Pacific Northwest but was raised in the South. After graduating from the University of Alabama, she taught school for 40 years. In 1994, she founded Hill Creek Christian School in Mount Vernon, Washington. Throughout her career, the subject she most enjoyed teaching was creative writing.

After Patty and her husband completed a year living in their cabin on Dunn Mountain in the Huckleberry Range of Northeastern Washington they moved back to Alabama where she is writing a devotional of short inspirational pieces and poetry. Her other hobbies include meeting with her Christian writers' group (Pond and Parchment Guild) via Zoom, spending time with friends and family, watching wildlife, and taking long walks with her Labrador Retriever, Liberty.

Award-winning author, speaker, and blogger **Penny L. Hunt** (p. 68) has been published in *Chicken Soup for the Soul*, *Guideposts*, *The Upper Room,* 12 of the 13 books in the *Short and Sweet* series, and online in *Just Eighteen Summers*. Her most recent book, *Bounce! Don't Break…* helps others recover from setbacks. *Little White Squirrel's Secret — A Special Place to Practice,* is an Amazon.com bestseller children's book dedicated to her severely-autistic granddaughter.

Penny lives in the rural-peach-growing region of South Carolina with her husband, Bill, a retired career naval officer and attaché, and their two dogs. While she enjoys gardening and gourmet cooking, her greatest passion is to lead others to a personal and intimate relationship with Christ. Visit her at PennyLHunt.com.

Debbie Jansen (p. 85) earned a degree in psychology from Evangel University, where she met Ron and began their marriage of 50 years. They have three children and seven grandchildren. Debbie has written four books, and her articles have been published in *Today's Christian Woman* and *Focus on the Family*. She has also appeared on radio and television. She founded and writes curriculum for The Family Training Center. As a minister and speaker, she creates videos for YouTube and produces a podcast on Spotify. You can view her classes for Moms for America at: www.momsforamerica.us.

Debbie collects stories, information, and best friends. While she loves sharing her rollercoaster of life, she is also mesmerized by the adventures of others. Always the optimist, she expects to find answers to every difficult situation. Visit her at www.debbiejansen.com.

Lillian Joyce (p. 36) is the author of the blog, *Ponderings of a Potted Plant,* where she turns everyday experiences into stories using a mix of poems and prose. Born in New York, Joyce spent her growing up years in the Middle East. She enjoyed the sand and the mountains before finally moving to the deep South in the United States.

Following her childhood dream, she later boarded the ship *Africa Mercy* and traveled with it to different parts of West Africa. Using these multicultural experiences, she enjoys writing poetry in the form of stories that mix and match different cultural traditions. In addition to writing and exploring, she can be found deep in thought while sitting on the couch, looking out the window and watching the rain drip down the glass. Read her work at https://pottedplantponders.blogspot.com.

Married to Cary for 44 years, **Liz Kimmel** (p. 97), has two children and four grandchildren. She has published two books of Christian prose/poetry and a grammar workbook for middle-school students. She has contributed to all of the *Short and Sweet* books. Her devotions are included in Guideposts' *All God's Creatures* from 2020–2024. She has a fiction piece in *Seasons of Change,* an anthology of the Minnesota Christian Writers Guild. Her new book, *Putting Punch in the Parables,* is a photo-  illustrated, alliterative retelling of ten of the parables of Jesus.

When not writing, Liz provides admin support for four non-profits (Dare to Believe, Great Commission Media Ministries, Minnesota House of Prayer, and the Minnesota Christian Writers Guild). Visit her website at https://www.lizkimmelwordwright.com.

Debra Kornfield (p. 80) published four books in 20 years of mission work in Brazil while pioneering abuse recovery and raising four children. She framed her memoir, *Karis: All I See Is Grace* (now also in Portuguese and Spanish), around her daughter Karis's luminous journals and poetry. *Horse Thief 1898, Treasure Hunt 1904* and *Facing the Faeries 1906,* published in February 2024, complete the Charlie and Cally trilogy.

To commemorate 10 years since Karis died, Debra is bringing to life  several children's books they wrote together. Living now in Pittsburgh, Pennsylvania, Debra enjoys adventuring with her four grandchildren, hiking, and keeping up with her husband, Dave, her seven siblings, and many South American friends. Whenever she can, Debra also returns to Latin America. Follow her on HorseThief1898.blog and devotionally on ButGod.blog.

Jim Layton (p. 103) attended New Hampshire College, University of Maine, and Husson University. He served in the United States Navy for 22 years, retiring as a Senior Chief Cryptologic Technician. After his naval retirement, he was employed as a town manager and became a Maine state legislator. He retired again in 2004.

Jim is married to Valerie, a former Navy Lieutenant who worked primarily in Nuclear Weapons and Naval Intelligence. They love to travel and have visited 80 countries on six continents. The Laytons are avid collectors of art — primarily the early Masters, the 19th-Century Hudson River School, and religious artwork by Chagall. They collect ancient artifacts, dating back to 750 BC. They are active in church work and pro-life ministry. He enjoys golfing, antiquing, and giving his friends a hard time.

John Leatherman (p. 116) is a writer, editor, cartoonist, writing-contest judge, word-puzzle creator, and escape-room designer. He is a longtime member and former officer of Word Weavers International, where he mentors writers, leads occasional seminars on self-editing, and writes a long-running grammar blog. He has won numerous writing awards from Word Weavers International, American Christian Fiction Writers, and other organizations. He has worked with over a dozen authors to edit, proofread, rewrite, and revise their manuscripts for publication. He also served as Communications Editor for Recode Media. His writing credits include book reviews for *Christian Retailing*, scripts for Shoestring Radio Theater, devotionals for *Keys for Kids*, and cartoons for several magazines. He maintains a secret identity as a mild-mannered software consultant who lives in Florida and has two kids and a dog.

Allyson West Lewis (p. 105) is an award-winning author. After more than 20 years as an institutional director on Wall Street and a business developer for an IT networking company, she turned to her childhood love — writing. Allyson has been published in multiple *Short and Sweet* books including *What's In a Name? Everything!* and *When the World Wore Masks*. She's written two speculative fiction books, and has published blog posts, short stories, and articles in literary magazines and anthologies.

Besides teaching life skills to desperate pre-teen parents, Allyson has facilitated leadership training, served as a one-on-one mentor, and led a women's small group. She enjoys playing tennis and walking her dogs on the beach. She loves her amazing husband, sons, and grandchildren. Allyson writes from Hilton Head Island, South Carolina, with a Golden Retriever and an irascible terrier sprawled at her feet.

Russell MacClaren (p. 45) landed in New Orleans at age five when his father became a professor at LSU. The city, its music, cuisine, culture and history welcomed the young family. Russell has been a member of the clergy, church choirs, scouts, athletics, art, weight lifting, airborne military combat, construction, and many genres of writing: poetry, children's stories, flash fiction, short stories, novels and songs.

Russell's experience includes participation in several groups — founding two himself — editing for an online magazine, speaking on zoom and open mics, reading on public television, sponsoring and winning contests, conducting events and workshops, and sitting on the board of poetry societies. Now retired and living in New Orleans, he's compiled three books of personal poetry and is published in anthologies around the country.

Author and speaker **Terry Magness** (p. 125) is the founder of Grace Harbour Ministries, a biblically based teaching and discipleship ministry to the nations. She is passionate to help others know the character of God and who they are in Christ and to live victorious lives and grow to maturity in Christ, filled with His Spirit.

As an ordained Assembly of God minister, her experience in counseling and as a coach equips her to undergird and strengthen pastors and their wives, as well as credentialed women in ministry, and to encourage and empower the church.

Terry enjoys writing, photography, art, and fishing with her husband, Don. Their daughter Valarie, son Greg, daughter-in-law Jean Anne, and three granddaughters — Fallon, Savannah, and Kendall — keep them amazed, delighted, and ever thankful.

Karen Masteller (p. 130) — formerly a private-school language-arts teacher for 25 years — now employs the art of language to share faith, humor, and encouragement with her readers. Her writings include devotions, poems, children's stories, memoirs, novels, and non-fiction pieces. She is also the caretaker of five novels in progress, and all of the characters are calling.

Finding herself on the other side of the teacher's desk, she is eager to learn and to improve her writing. As a student of the craft, she attends writers' conferences, connects with critique groups, reads instructional material, and maintains membership in Word Weavers International to stoke the creative fires. Transplanted from Pennsylvania, Karen now lives in the countryside southeast of Nashville, Tennessee — a quiet spot conducive to pondering and writing.

Cristina Moore (p. 13) was born in Puerto Rico and grew up in Tennessee. Currently, she lives in North Carolina with her husband of over 25 years and her two younger children, twins Hope and Helena. She is the owner and CEO of Bronze Star Homes, an employee at Duke Energy, and currently serves in the North Carolina National Guard as a Brigadier General.

Cristina served as an elder in her church and loves teaching Bible study. She celebrates God's Word by sharing the grace and miracles both she and her husband have witnessed through multiple combat deployments and their call to serve their community and country. In her spare time, Cristina places family as a priority and is enjoying returning to her passion of writing and touching the lives of those reading her words.

For over 30 years, **Alice H. Murray** (p. 39) practiced as an adoption attorney in Florida. Currently she works as Operations Manager for End Game Press and pursues her passion for writing. She writes a weekly blog tinged with humor (aliceinwonderingland.wordpress.com), a weekly faith column (Feet To Faith) on patheos.com, and three devotions a month for Dynamic Women In Missions' Facebook page.

Alice's work has been published in several books in the *Short and Sweet* series, *Chicken Soup For The Soul*, *Guideposts* publications, and compilation works. She is a regular contributor to *GO!* Magazine, a quarterly Christian magazine published in the Florida Panhandle. Alice's first book, *The Secret Of Chimneys,* an annotated Agatha Christie work, was released in April 2023. Alice is the current president of the Destin Word Weavers Chapter.

Michelle Newman (p. 93) has always loved words, dating back to childhood when she wrote the story of a pocket who learns that pride goes before a fall when it gets splattered with spaghetti sauce! With a degree in history, she naturally leans toward non-fiction writing but loves fiction in all genres.

Her creativity finds daily outlet through teaching at a small Christian school. She enjoys encouraging a love of reading among her students and researching history that might interest her middle-schoolers. When not teaching, Michelle takes day trips with friends, hunts for books for her classroom, and works on a non-fiction manuscript about the sanctification God is working in her through prolonged, unsolicited singleness. She can be found on Instagram @wrestlingwithsingleness.

Beverly Robertson (p. 52) recalls that her high school English class first sparked her interest in writing. Fellow students selected her essay, "Teachers," to be published in the local paper. Stories smoldered in a file cabinet until her retirement as a teacher's aide in an elementary school. Then her writing ignited.

She pulled out her stories on biblical women, put them together in an anthology, and self-published the book *Bible Brides: Trials and Triumphs*. For her church women's group, she presented a monthly lesson on different women of the Bible. She had a short story appear in *Whatever Lovely* magazine and Christmas stories in *Celebrating Christmas* and *Christmas Spirit*. She networks and also hones her writing skills as a member of the American Christian Fiction Writers.

Kim Robinson (p. 132) just loves Jesus! It's fun for her to see His "kisses" from heaven — the ways in which He touches her day with helps, gifts, wise words, and friends. For years she taught grades 6-12, mostly English and math, in Oregon and Alaska. Then God called her to a hospital ship that served West African ports with hope and free surgeries. She taught the missionary children onboard, again, mostly English and Bible, from 2007-2020, when COVID-19 shut the work down.

Today, Kim lives in Oregon where she hikes, sews quilts, and reads (a lot). Her daughter's family in Montana and her son from LA delight her. A member of Cascade Christian Writers, Kim writes for a number of devotion magazines and often serves missionaries as their editor.

Michael Shoemaker (p. 100) is a poet, photographer and writer from Magna, Utah. He is the author of a poetry/photography collection, *Rocky Mountain Reflections,* (Poets' Choice) and the forthcoming *Grasshoppers in the Field.* Michael is a winner of the California State Poetry Society Prize, is on the shortlist for The Letter Review Prize for Poetry, and also in the anthology of the Rio Grande Valley International Poetry Festival.

Michael has been awarded a 2024 grant by the Utah Division of Arts and Museums for his poetry. His writing has appeared in *Blue Lake Review, Literary Revelations Journal,* The *High Window, Seashores Haiku Journal, The Penwood Review,* and also in anthologies at *Poetry Pacific, Pure Slush,* and *Echoes of the Wild.* He lives with his family in Utah where every day he enjoys looking out on the Great Salt Lake.

Desiree St. Clair Spears (p. 49) has written for numerous publications including Guideposts, A *Joy-Full Season*, *Connections*, *The Times-Crescent* newspaper, and her church blog. Her work has also been published in six books in the *Short and Sweet* series. She earned her M.A. at Notre Dame of Maryland University and her B.S. at Salisbury University. A recently-retired high school career-and-technology-education teacher, Desiree has 30 years of experience teaching all ages.

She is active in her church serving as trustee, greeter, and leader of a women's small group. Desiree recently celebrated her second anniversary with her husband, Robert, and is the mother of three adult children and grandmother of eleven. In addition to spoiling the grandkids, she enjoys traveling, hiking, gardening, and life on the farm. Her blog can be accessed at http://desireeglass.blogspot.com.

Judson I. Stone (p. 54) is a volunteer at the Walton Correctional Institution Florida, Bible study leader, and avid beachcomber. He is a retired pastor, corporate chaplain, and Fellowship of Christian Athletes volunteer sports chaplain. He self-published biographies of his great-great-uncle *A Modest But Crucial Hero: The Life and Legacy of Rev. George E. Stone (1873-1899)* and his father *A Last Chapter of the Greatest Generation*. He is working on a biography of a great uncle including a transcription of his World War I diary. Judson is a member of the Destin Word Weavers International. He collects belt buckles and old documents.

Judson is married, the father of three sons, and Pop-pop to five grandchildren. He and his wife reside in Santa Rosa Beach, Florida.

For over 25 years, **Jan White** (p. 128) has written a weekly religion column that appears in the *Andalusia Star-News* and the *Enterprise Southeast Sun*, as well as other newspapers. In 2020, she published a compilation of her columns in a book titled *Everyday Faith for Daily Life*.

Among her numerous writing awards, Jan received the prestigious Amy Writing Award for one of her columns selected among submissions from writers nationwide. Her articles and devotionals have been published in *Focus on the Family, Charisma Magazine,* and other publications. Jan has worked for three newspapers and written articles for two ministries. She and her husband, Greg, live in Andalusia, Alabama, where she is active as a community volunteer and loves being Grandma Jan to two granddaughters.

Following the background of **Kenneth Avon White** (p. 90) is like trying to connect the dots on a Dalmatian. His "day-job" writing life has spanned the worlds of radio-and-television advertising, public relations, and corporate communications. His personal writing career did not begin until 2013 with devotionals published in *The Upper Room* magazine. From there, Ken has been published in every book in the *Short and Sweet* series and several compilations from *Guideposts*.

An organizational-change manager, Ken has also worked as a book publicist, media-relations practitioner, independent film producer, technical writer, and business analyst.

Ken is a graduate of American University and resides in the Charlotte, North Carolina area. He spends his spare time taking in the performance arts, playing cards with friends, and making day trips to spots so tucked away they befuddle GPS systems.

Susan Cheeves King

For nearly four decades, Susan King (p. 107) has been a fish out of water — a big extrovert serving in professions dominated by introverts: writer, college teacher, and editor. During her nearly 25 years as an editor with *The Upper Room* magazine, Susan taught and mentored writers at over 100 Christian writers' conferences in the U.S. and Canada.

While teaching English and feature-writing classes over a span of 27 years at Lipscomb, Biola, and Abilene Christian Universities, her greatest challenge and joy was to help each of her over 4,000 students become the epitome of an educated person: someone who can think well, speak well, and write well.

These days, she pursues her passion through Susan King Editorial Services (www.susankingedits.com) by editing and mentoring writers and also by teaching and helping writers perfect their craft at writers' conferences. She and husband, Joe, live in middle Tennessee — very close to two of their grown children and their two grandsons.

If you enjoyed

We Hold These Truths

you might also enjoy
other books in the *Short and Sweet* Series

Short and Sweet
Small Words for Big Thoughts

Short and Sweet Too
More Small Words for Big Thoughts

The Short and Sweet of It
When the Right Word Is a Short Word

Short and Sweet Goes Fourth

Short and Sweet Takes the Fifth

Family Album

A Different Beat

Humili8ing
Tales We Wish Weren't True

Angels in Disguise?

What's in a Name? Everything!

When the World Wore Masks

Mishaps and Misadventures

www.ingramcontent.com/pod-product-compliance
Lightning Source LLC
Chambersburg PA
CBHW060538100426
42743CB00009B/1561